Advancing Equity-Focused School Counseling for All Students

Using author narratives, this book brings attention to racial disparities that currently exist in schools within the historical context of pivotal legal cases in America while emphasizing the importance of assessing and supporting students through a culturally appropriate lens that recognizes student strengths.

The authors provide current and historical frameworks through which school counselors can develop a more socially just and liberation-orientated school counseling program. These frameworks center and unveil the ways in which social rank, segregation, and racism influence development, particularly for Black and Brown children. The book underscores the value of community partnerships and the role of strategic partnerships to support a college culture, particularly for student populations with historically limited access to higher education. Readers will also learn about misconceptions of racially and ethnically minoritized children and the related impacts on misdiagnosis and overrepresentation in special education.

School counselors looking to ensure equity and social justice within their classrooms, analyze their own privilege, and support students of all backgrounds will find this timely text indispensable in creating a program that fosters understanding and growth.

Sam Steen holds a PhD in Counselor Education and is a Licensed Professional School Counselor in Virginia.

Shekila Melchior holds a PhD in Counselor Education and is a Licensed Professional Counselor in Virginia.

Amber Brenae Sansbury-Scott, M.Ed. and PhD Candidate in Education, investigates family engagement with Head Start teachers and families.

"This amazing gem of a book integrates the fields of school counseling and the educational and developmental sciences in its strengths-based focus on racial and ethnically minoritized people, with a historical focus that simultaneously provides an action plan to identify and address racial and ethnic disparities."

Pamela W. Garner, *Professor of Childhood Studies in the School of Integrative Studies and Human Development and Family Science at George Mason University*

"This book is a must-read for school counselors interested in building a deeper understanding of students of Color and their experiences within systemically racist school systems. With an impressive scope, Steen, Melchior, & Sansbury have unapologetically centered the voices, experiences, and cultural assets of students of Color in PreK-12 Schools. The body of work within this book has the potential to inform school counseling programs, policies, and practices that promote equity and opportunities for all students. And "all students" means "all students," including those historically marginalized."

Joseph M. Williams, *Professor, Counselor Education, and Supervision, University of North Carolina – Chapel Hill*

"This book provides concrete strategies and information that will be helpful for students in a school counseling program. The chapters are succinct, easy to read, yet full of important information that will be useful to any school counselor in training who wants to adopt an antiracist mindset and effect change for racialized and marginalized populations."

Dr. Dana Griffin, *Associate Professor, Associate Editor, Professional School Counseling, School of Education, The University of North Carolina at Chapel Hill*

Advancing Equity-Focused School Counseling for All Students

Confronting Disproportionality across PreK-12 Schools

Sam Steen, Shekila Melchior, and Amber Brenae Sansbury-Scott

Routledge
Taylor & Francis Group

NEW YORK AND LONDON

Designed cover image by: © Getty Images

First published 2024
by Routledge
605 Third Avenue, New York, NY 10158

and by Routledge
4 Park Square, Milton Park, Abingdon, Oxon, OX14 4RN

Routledge is an imprint of the Taylor & Francis Group, an informa business

© 2024 Sam Steen, Shekila Melchior, and Amber Brenae Sansbury-Scott

ISBN: 978-1-032-12790-3 (hbk)
ISBN: 978-1-032-12788-0 (pbk)
ISBN: 978-1-003-22625-3 (ebk)

DOI: 10.4324/9781003226253

Typeset in Times New Roman
by MPS Limited, Dehradun

Contents

Foreword

A persistent and pervasive conviction held by many within the field of school counseling is the indispensability of proficiency; specifically, the idea that a professional school counselor's success is predicated primarily on the ability to observe, learn and model, refine, and master the very intricate and technical clinical counseling skills common to the field. This idea is reflected in the fact that the impetus for the creation of the profession was the urgent need to develop a cadre of counseling professionals who possessed a unique skillset to objectively identify the most intelligent, qualified, and capable students for post-secondary education and careers. While clinical proficiency is certainly an important facet in becoming an effective school counseling professional, a rigid, myopic focus on the acquisition of technical skills overshadows how vital it is for school counseling professionals, regardless of tenure, to attend to the symbiotic interplay of individual, social/societal, cultural, and institutional dynamics that permeate and encapsulate the counseling endeavor as it unfolds within the context of the K-12 American education system.

Attending to this symbiotic interplay has been evidenced in the shift in the educational discourse of the 1980s and 1990s towards culturally relevant pedagogy, the emergence of multicultural competencies in the 1990s, and the endorsement of multicultural and social justice perspectives and frameworks by the most prominent school counseling governing body, the American School Counseling Association. The current sociopolitical milieu, where books written by renowned Black, queer, and endarkened intellectuals are being banned and physically removed from K-12 school libraries and where trans-students are being socially and physically antagonized, requires school counselors who are knowledgeable about the historical and contemporary plight of these students and not merely those professionals espousing a commitment to clinical proficiency. Encouraging preservice and in-service school counselors to eschew the allure to prioritize proficiency and to attend to the intersectional nature of institutional and structural dynamics of race, gender, culture, and ableness exemplifies what it means to be an exemplary professional school counselor educator.

In this book, Steen, Melchior, and Sansbury offer a rich and robust contribution to the school counseling profession, a narrative that provides a historically accurate and comprehensive overview of the origins of the field. This book consistently invites the reader to engage in ongoing self-reflection and to consider what role they might take in reshaping the discipline and profession moving forward. Steen, Melchior, and Sansbury have managed to compose a readable and widely accessible text, one that is appropriate for even the most unseasoned novice in the field, without compromising depth or rigor. Each chapter includes lengthy operational definitions, reflection questions, experiential activities or vignettes, and, occasionally, adaptable templates that school counseling professionals can immediately modify and apply. And yet, as significant as these attributes of the text are, the most meaningful contribution this text makes to the school counseling nomenclature is how the authors deliberately and intentionally engage equity and social justice and how they each use autobiography to illuminate what those terms and concepts have meant and continue to mean to the school experiences of Black students and students of color. Through narrative and autobiography, approaches that are being embraced by professional school counselors with increasing regularity, Steen, Melchior, and Sansbury not only demonstrate how the remnants and legacies of slavery and Jim Crow continue to reverberate in the lives of Black students and students of color, but why it is unconscionable for school counseling programs to continually graduate students who are unwilling to act as agents of systemic change. Steen, Melchior, and Sansbury's book is a useful and important addition to the school counseling discourse and can be used as a primary or supplementary text for several professional school counseling courses. That versatility makes Steen, Melchior, and Sansbury's book an important asset to professional school counselor educators and school counseling students alike.

Ahmad R. Washington, Ph.D.
he/him/his
Associate Professor Department of Pan-African Studies
College of Arts and Sciences Department of
Counseling and Human Development
College of Education and Human Development
The University of Louisville

Preface

We believe we are change agents; therefore, we must intentionally prepare professional school counselors to engage in equitable practices. Professional school counselors can use a focused cultural lens to foster environments of inclusive excellence. We invite the reader to consider a broader, interconnected perspective of schools (e.g., staff), children (e.g., students across early childhood–Grade 12), and families (e.g., parents, grandparents, extended and kinship networks, and primary caretakers') experiences, and the authors' own personal and professional challenges and successes navigating the nation's public schools. We desire to focus singularly on Black and Brown children and adolescents throughout this book to include the voices and strengths of students who have been historically excluded from the school counseling conversation for far too long.

In 2021, more than 30,000 school counselors were surveyed on their knowledge of race and racism and its impact on the students they serve. Fewer than 50% indicated having a comprehensive understanding of diverse populations. This book aims to merge the gaps among school counselor knowledge, practice, and cultural competency. The book centers on the strengths of Black, African American, and racial/ethnic minoritized people. As school counselors, we no longer want to contribute to the erasure of student narratives that have been relegated to multicultural add-ons and deficit language. This book will celebrate, highlight, and center these students, yet it is applicable to all students.

Council for Accreditation of Counseling and Related Educational Program (CACREP) Standards

CACREP Standard	Chapter within the text that corresponds CACREP Standard
Legal and ethical considerations specific to school counseling (CACREP 5.G.2.n)	This standard is addressed in Chapter 10
Development of school counseling program mission statements and objectives (CACREP 5.G.3.a)	This standard is addressed in Chapter 5
Design and evaluation of school counseling programs (CACREP 5.G.3.b)	This standard is addressed in Chapters 1 and 5
Core curriculum design, lesson plan development, classroom management strategies, and differentiated instructional strategies (CACREP 5.G.3.c)	This standard is part of Chapters 5 and 7
Interventions to promote academic development (CACREP 5.G.3.d)	This standard is part of Chapters 5 and 7
Strategies to facilitate school and postsecondary transitions (CACREP 5.G.3.g)	This standard is part of Chapter 6
Skills to critically examine the connections between social, familial, emotional, and behavior problems and academic achievement (CACREP 5.G.3.h)	This standard is part of Chapters 7 and 8

(Continued)

CACREP Standard	Chapter within the text that corresponds CACREP Standard
Approaches to increase promotion and graduation rates (CACREP 5.G.3.i)	This standard is part of Chapter 6
Interventions to promote college and career readiness (CACREP 5.G.3.j)	This standard is part of Chapters 5 and 6
Strategies to promote equity in student achievement and college access (CACREP 5.G.3.k)	This standard is part of Chapter 6
Techniques to foster collaboration and teamwork within schools (CACREP 5.G.3.l)	This standard is part of Chapter 7
Strategies for implementing and coordinating peer intervention programs (CACREP 5.G.3.m)	This standard is part of Chapter 7
Use of accountability data to inform decision making (CACREP 5.G.3.n)	This standard is part of Chapters 5 and 9
Use of data to advocate for programs and students (CACREP 5.G.3.o)	This standard is part of Chapters 1, 5, 6 and 9

American School Counseling Association (ASCA) Standards for School Counselor Preparation

ASCA Standards for School Counselor Preparation Programs	Chapter(s) associated with ASCA Standards for SC Prep Programs
1.1 Describe the organizational structure, governance, and evolution of the American education system as well as cultural, political, and social influences on current educational practices and on individual and collective learning environments.	Ch. 3
1.2 Describe the evolution of the school counseling profession, the basis for a comprehensive school counseling program, and the school counselor's role in supporting growth and learning for all students.	Ch. 5
1.3 Describe aspects of human development, such as cognitive, language, social/emotional, and physical development, as well as the impact of environmental stressors and societal inequities on learning and life outcomes.	Ch. 2
2.1 Describe established and emerging counseling and educational methods, including but not limited to childhood and adolescent development, learning theories, behavior modification and classroom management, social justice, multiculturalism, group counseling, college/career readiness, and crisis response.	Chs. 4, 6, 8
2.2 Demonstrate strengths-based counseling and relationship-building skills to support student growth and promote equity and inclusion.	Ch. 5

(Continued)

ASCA Standards for School Counselor Preparation Programs	Chapter(s) associated with ASCA Standards for SC Prep Programs
2.3 Describe established and emerging counseling theories and evidence-based techniques that are effective in a school setting, including but not limited to rational emotive behavior therapy, reality therapy, cognitive-behavioral therapy, Adlerian, solution-focused brief counseling, person-centered counseling, and family systems.	
3.1 Use multiple data points, including student interviews, direct observation, educational records, consultation with parents/families/staff, and test results to systematically identify student needs and collaboratively establish goals.	Ch. 7
3.2 Identify research-based individual counseling, group counseling, and classroom instruction techniques to promote academic achievement, college/career readiness, and social/emotional development for every student.	Chs. 5, 6
3.3 Demonstrate digital literacy and appropriate use of technology to track student progress, communicate effectively with stakeholders, analyze data, and assess student outcomes.	Ch. 10
4.1 Plan, organize and implement various instructional and counseling strategies as part of a comprehensive school counseling program (direct and indirect student services) to improve preK-12 student attitudes, knowledge, and skills.	Ch. 5
4.2 Collaborate with stakeholders such as families, teachers, support personnel, administrators, and community partners to create learning environments that promote educational equity, and support the success and well-being of every student.	Ch. 7
4.3 Describe how to access school and community resources to make appropriate referrals based on the needs of students.	Ch. 7
4.4 Demonstrate pedagogical skills, including culturally responsive classroom management strategies, lesson planning, and personalized instruction.	Ch. 5

(Continued)

ASCA Standards for School Counselor Preparation Programs	Chapter(s) associated with ASCA Standards for SC Prep Programs
5.1 Use data and student standards, such as the ASCA Mindsets and Behaviors for Student Success and appropriate state standards, to create school counseling program goals and action plans aligned with school improvement plans.	Ch. 5
5.2 Use process, perception, and outcome data, program and needs assessments, and other survey tools to monitor and refine the school counseling program.	Ch. 5
5.3 Use school-wide data to promote systemic change within the school so every student is prepared for post-secondary success.	Ch. 6
6.1 Explain the appropriate scope of practice for school counselors defined as the overall delivery of the comprehensive school counseling program, providing education, prevention, intervention, and referral services to students and their families.	Ch. 5
6.2 Demonstrate leadership, advocacy, and collaboration for the promotion of student learning and achievement, the school counseling program, and the profession.	Ch. 5
6.3 Engage in local, state, and national professional growth and development opportunities and demonstrate an emerging professional identity as a school counselor.	Ch. 7
7.1 Engage in professional behavior that reflects ASCA Ethical Standards for School Counselors and relevant federal and state laws and district policies.	Ch. 9
7.2 Describe the impact of federal and state laws and regulations and district policies on schools, students, families, and school counseling practice.	Ch. 2 and 9
7.3 Seek consultation and supervision to support ongoing critical reflection to identify cultural blind spots and prevent ethical lapses.	Ch. 7 and 9

Self-Evaluation

Instructions: Please complete this self-evaluation, which includes a list of "I believe" statements, at least two times. First, take this assessment prior to reading the book to gain a sense of your current understanding of Black students and their families within a school counseling context. Second, complete this assessment again after your reading. You can rate yourself using the 6-point scale. Be sure to tally your score at the end. Compare the totals and take note of your ongoing growth.

Strongly Disagree (SD) = 1	Disagree (D) = 2	
Somewhat Disagree (SWD) = 3	Somewhat Agree (SWA) = 4	
Agree (A) = 5	Strongly Agree (SA) = 6	

		SD	D	SWD	SWA	A	SA
1.	I believe school integration is a good idea and segregation is problematic.	1	2	3	4	5	6
2.	I believe school policymakers and officials need to emphasize funding schools equitably.	1	2	3	4	5	6
3.	I believe Black communities provide assets for school policies, administrators, teachers, and staff.	1	2	3	4	5	6
4.	I believe school counseling practice should intentionally examine the impact of race on Black children in schools.	1	2	3	4	5	6

(Continued)

		SD	D	SWD	SWA	A	SA
5.	I believe school counselors must build school-community partnerships that can help explore the strengths of Black communities and the within-group differences	1	2	3	4	5	6
6.	I believe it is important to recruit Black individuals to consider the field of school counseling as a career.	1	2	3	4	5	6
7.	I believe the infusion of Black culture within pedagogy for school counselor trainees can further develop their understanding of the potential for Black excellence within these students.	1	2	3	4	5	6
8.	I believe school counselors and other educators must understand how school curricula, policies, and procedures support racism.	1	2	3	4	5	6
9.	I believe as a school counselor, I can support Black students by collaboratively developing strong school-family-community partnerships.	1	2	3	4	5	6
10.	I believe all school counselors and educators need to develop their racial identity.	1	2	3	4	5	6
11.	I believe I can explain the need and generate ideas for deepening awareness of racial identity to combat racist attitudes.	1	2	3	4	5	6
12.	I believe I understand racial identity development and how it might be applied to Black students and families.	1	2	3	4	5	6
13.	I believe I can strengthen the relationships within schools that include Black students and families using my unique personal traits.	1	2	3	4	5	6

(Continued)

		SD	D	SWD	SWA	A	SA
14.	I believe I can advocate for structural changes in schools by examining policies and practices that may negatively impact Black students and families.	1	2	3	4	5	6
15.	I believe I seek opportunities to gain further education about the Black community's strengths by attending conferences, professional development seminars, and continuing education courses.	1	2	3	4	5	6
16.	I believe that highlighting and affirming the voices of Black students and families is the foundation of advocacy.	1	2	3	4	5	6
17.	I believe I can educate myself about the cultural practices of Black students and families by understanding the role that racial and cultural socialization plays in early child development.	1	2	3	4	5	6
18.	I believe it is important to acquire an in-depth contextual understanding of Black families' cultural practices.	1	2	3	4	5	6
19.	I believe that school counselors can create inclusive and equitable environments for students and families whose racial and cultural backgrounds span the intersectionality framework.	1	2	3	4	5	6
20.	I believe I can describe future actions for combating inequities in schools while advocating on behalf of Black students and families.	1	2	3	4	5	6
Total Score Notes							

Part I

History, Identity, and Advocacy

Describing Equity within Schools

Chapter 1

Introduction

Developing a Framework for Action

Author Narrative: Sam Steen

In July of 2009, while attending a family reunion in Greenwood, Mississippi, I read a headline titled *"The State of Mississippi has Never Been Able to Educate Black Men."* My mother was born in Greenwood. Shortly after high school, she married my father, who was from a neighboring county. Greenwood and Clarksdale were considered impoverished, rural communities. Aside from a few exceptions, the education system had limited resources as a result of poverty and entrenched systemic racism. At the time I had earned a Ph.D. and made the transition from a full-time professional school counselor of nearly ten years to a full-time professor at a university in Washington, DC. I reflected on how fortunate it was that my father joined the military, taking us out of Mississippi. From the time I was born up to the age of 13 years old, I lived in numerous states domestically and in Germany. I wondered if my educational experiences would have been quite different had I been educated in Mississippi for my entire upbringing. I ponder this knowing the truth about Emmitt Till who was a 14-year-old Black boy kidnaped, beaten, and lynched in Mississippi in 1955 based on a misunderstanding and a narrative of lies that ensued.

Content

Moving Past Discomfort by Discovering and Expressing Oneself

This current book is written for school counselors from all racial identities. And, if this discomfort applies to you, then it is time to get over this discomfort. School counselors are skilled at handling tense situations. While the majority of school counselors in the US are White, they are not all White. Discussing race need not be a negative activity. Exploring Blackness within the school counseling context should be a

DOI: 10.4324/9781003226253-2

positive experience, although emphatically this has not always been the case. Exploring White privilege is not enough. Moving beyond what discrepancies exist is important. Day-Vines et al. (2013) found characteristics that influence a counselor's willingness to discuss race included beliefs about the importance of discussing race and culture, lack of knowledge on broaching race and culture, previous experiences, skill set, self-efficacy, racial identity functioning, and multicultural competence. These authors continue to develop a promising and user-friendly conceptual framework called the Broaching Model, which school counselors can draw upon to engage in their practice. The Broaching Model is applicable across disciplines (Day-Vines et al., 2021) but especially relevant in school settings. Broaching race, ethnicity, and culture early and often fosters a connection between the students, colleagues, families, and school counselors. School counselors can incorporate broaching in all of their interactions; however, their intersections of identity must be taken into account before having these courageous conversations. How one identifies themselves racially and expresses themselves culturally will impact these encounters. Racial critical consciousness will be discussed further in Chapter 3.

Discovering areas for growth and investment could prove to produce meaningful dividends. It is most critical to find ways to communicate honestly and openly regarding race and other salient issues. It will necessitate taking a conscious and consistent amount of effort and practice. In recent years the concept of compassionate communication has emerged in Diversity, Equity, and Inclusion spaces. The concept of compassionate communication encourages individuals to engage in dialogs nurtured by psychological safety. Compassionate communication is a skillful communication practice that encourages authentic and compassionate communication while remaining grounded in the space of difficult dialogs.

School Counseling training programs over the years have failed to encourage direct conversations related to race. In the past, it was noted that the reason Black and Brown students were not achieving success or overcoming achievement gaps was due to racial issues coupled with other developmental considerations. Should the burden be on the students to overcome these difficulties? There are numerous school counseling texts where the term "race" or "racism" cannot be found within the index (Baker & Gerler, 2008; Studer, 2015). Of course, other texts do include discussions of race and racism, but in a cursory fashion. Preparation programs for school counselors have not made significant strides in the training curriculum. Counselor educators use other resources in addition to textbooks and scholarly articles to supplement their teaching. The truth remains that schools uphold systems of racism because our larger society is grounded in systemic racism. It is essential to embrace opportunities for exploring race within the school counseling field. If school counselors want to become more familiar with engaging in the battle for equity and inclusion, it will be essential to prepare. Preparation is an ongoing process. In the following chapters, we provide the knowledge and skills needed. We will continue to provide opportunities for self-reflection. In Chapter 2, we briefly explain the history of education and the interplay of racism and discrimination in schools.

School counselors are change agents. School counselors actively support all students in their academic, social/emotional, and college/career development and pursuits. Although the authors place heavy emphasis on Black and Brown students in this literature, when we refer to students, we mean *all* students. But, what if you work in a school that is made up primarily of students who identify as White? First, your intersections of identity need to be examined. Next, we believe race, gender, class, and other aspects of the identity of your students must be acknowledged. Identity is so complex that it is necessary to remember that even in a school where it appears that all of the students share a racial identity, there are often singletons (i.e., at least one student) in those schools who may not feel seen or heard. One student holding a unique identity stands to receive the same benefits as others holding their special qualities. No one person is more important than the rest. We all deserve to be free, thrive and flourish. The role of a school counselor is to engage all students – individually, in small and large groups, and across comprehensive programming efforts. School counselors must know themselves, their interpersonal skills, and their navigation of multiple and multifaceted relationships, including the systems and environments in which these relationships occur. Such insight can help develop and communicate a school counseling philosophy. A good starting point is examining one's own culture, which includes race, gender, class, and other intersecting identities. How do these intersecting identities impact our lives and the students we serve? This awareness leads to helping *all* students.

School counseling involves important terminology and concepts that surface throughout the book that will be useful for school counselors to understand. We provide citations for some of these terms and concepts when appropriate. Other terms are defined by the authors, using their professional experiences to develop school counselors' understanding of these various concepts. In this textbook, we include *Key Terms* to reinforce the essential concepts, policies, and historical context to deepen readers' knowledge in related chapters. Within the categories below, readers will find broader definitions in alphabetical order:

Key Terms by Category

Equity-Focused School Counseling Terms

504 Plan

A 504 plan is a blueprint for how the school will support a student with a disability and remove barriers to learning. The goal is to provide the student with access to the learning environment and ensure academic success. Such plans should prevent discrimination and protect the rights of students with disabilities, as covered by Section 504 of the Rehabilitation Act. Accommodations and modifications can span environmental, organizational, behavioral, or presentation and evaluation strategies.

Adverse Childhood Experiences (ACEs)

Potentially traumatic events occurring during childhood (0–17). The impact of these events is often linked to mental illness, substance misuse, and chronic health problems.

American with Disabilities Act (ADA)

Federal disability anti-discrimination legislation, which was passed in 1990. The ADA guaranteed rights to individuals with disabilities in the areas of employment, transportation, government services, telecommunication, and public accommodations.

Black/Brown

Terms used to describe individuals who identify as non-White. In education research, this term increasingly refers to a coalition or shared experiences for students who identify as Black and Brown (e.g., African American, Caribbean, African, Latine, Asian, Native American, and Indigenous students).

Hispanic-Serving Institutions (HSIs)

The designation of Hispanic-Serving Institution (HSI) was in large part due to the Hispanic Association of Colleges and Universities in 1986, though the evolution of these institutions began in 1970. HSIs were recognized by the Higher Education Act in 1992. Unlike HBCUs and Tribal Colleges, the designation of HSIs was a result of the institution's proximity to large Hispanic populations and shifts in demographic populations. There are more than 200 HSIs across the United States.

Historically Black Colleges and Universities (HBCUs)

The formation of Historically Black Colleges and Universities (HBCUs) began in the mid-1800s, and until 1890 the Federal government granted land to Black Colleges and Universities. Prior to the desegregation of higher education institutions in the 1950s and 60s, Black students could attend only Black Colleges and Universities. It was not until 1965 that HBCUs were designated by the US Department of Education. There are more than 100 HBCUs in the United States, with the majority of them in the Southeast region of the country.

Individualized Education Program (IEP)

A legal document that includes a "plan" of action to ensure a student with an identified disability receives specialized instruction and additional services. IEPs are built upon by a special education law also known as the Individuals with Disabilities Education Act (IDEA). The IEP form/process will include details and discussions about foundational information in every case (e.g., factors requiring the IEP, present level of functioning academically and behaviorally, annual goals and progress, services and accommodation, assessments, school environment, and communication with parents/caregivers). Other information will include documentation of the services, meetings, consent, progress reports, and extensions if needed.

Intersectionality

This term describes how race, class, gender, and other individual characteristics "intersect" with one another and overlap (Crenshaw, 1991). It provides a lens to see where power comes and collides, where it interlocks and intersects with one's self, family, and community.

Though this analytical framework stemmed from Crenshaw's experiences advocating equity and justice with a civil rights lens, intersectionality can be used within schools to offer ways for students to view themselves and to challenge inconsistencies and imbalances that surface. School counselors addressing intersectionality can shine a light on strengths and disparities. From this, we can dismantle inequities by directly addressing them unapologetically.

Minority Serving Institutions (MSI)

Federally-recognized Title IV Colleges and Universities institutions that enroll high numbers of racial/ethnic minoritized students. The following are types of

MSIs: Historically Black Colleges & Universities (HBCU), Hispanic-Serving Institutions (HSI), and Tribal Colleges and Universities (TCU).

Race

An evolving group of "socially constructed categories that are assigned to individuals based on physical characteristics" (James et al., 2018, p. 420) like skin color, facial attributes, or hair texture. Examples include Black, Asian, Latine, White, Native American or Indigenous, biracial, and multiracial. In schools, race continues to be a politically laden term that suggests or implies some students perform better in certain activities (e.g., academics or sports) due to mental, physical, and behavioral characteristics that are innate. For example, students' demographic information is provided and race could be used to categorize and determine the level at which (e.g., academic, honors, special education) to place students. However, school counselors could help others understand and accept that race is a fundamental part of our identities and deserves to be acknowledged and appreciated, rather than used to separate, create division, or hold people back from reaching their true potential.

Racial/Ethnic Disproportionality

This phenomenon in school discipline occurs when a particular racial/ethnic group shows lower or higher rates of a particular school discipline outcome than a comparison racial/ethnic group. For instance, if school rates of police referral are two times higher among Native American students than among White students, this indicates that Native American students experience disproportionate rates of school discipline outcomes.

Racial Ethnic Minoritized

This term is used throughout the text in place of Racial Minority to combat racist language. *Racial Ethnic Minoritized* individuals can be seen as facing systemic barriers rather than be viewed through a lens of deficiency.

Racial Identity

This term refers to the attitudes, perceptions, and beliefs that one holds regarding their racial group and in relation to other racial groups (Swanson et al., 2003). Scholars have noted that the White population often has difficulty exploring race and whiteness (Helms, 2020). See the definition of whiteness below.

Racial Identity Development

This term represents a dynamic process of how individuals recognize, interpret, and assign value to one's racial self, others in and out of their racial group, and society as a "socially shared experience that is generated at the macro level" (Spencer et al., 2011, p. 469).

Racial Socialization

This term refers to ecological adaptations and an array of inter-generational processes that transmit attitudes, beliefs, and knowledge regarding racial group affiliation and intergroup dynamics (Hughes & Chen, 1997). Racial socialization may include family monitoring, social cues, cultural traditions, or modeled behaviors that cultivate an affirming sense of self and problem-solving skills. This racial socialization can occur for students across the racial spectrum.

Racism

This term refers to an entrenched and pervasive "system of oppression that results from a combination of prejudice and power. This combination produces institutional structures and social practices that deny equity to people based on race" at a micro or macro level (Cole & Verwayne, 2018). Manifestations include interpersonal racism, structural racism, institutional racism, internalized racism, cultural racism, and other less conspicuous but traumatic forms (i.e., microaggressions, racist stereotypes, racial harassment through destruction of property, defacing of Black cultural symbols or houses of worship, online stalking, etc.). In school settings, this volatile word essentially means racial domination in which the White culture is viewed as more favorable, worthy, etc, than non-White cultures. This idea is also used to justify the inequitable treatment or lower social positioning often experienced by other non-White racial groups. In schools, racism can emerge in many ways, but typically is institutional, internalized, or perceived, and can be covert (i.e., undercover, silent) or overt (i.e., obvious, aggressive) (Steen et al., 2023). For racism to disappear in schools, it must be eliminated within society. School counselors from all racial and cultural backgrounds can take responsibility for dealing with the impacts of racism. However, those who are particularly race-conscious can get others on board to increase the chances of mitigating the dire effects of racism.

Significant Disproportionality

This term is used to describe the widespread trend of students of certain racial and ethnic groups being misidentified for special education, placed in more restrictive educational settings, and disciplined at markedly higher rates than their peers. Due to bias within the education system (including within assessments and academic and other policies), Black and Brown students can be misidentified as needing special education, and are then placed in more restrictive settings and experience harsher discipline because of the intersectionality of race and special education – all of which can negatively affect student outcomes. "Significant disproportionality" ultimately refers to three separate but related trends that impact a student's educational experience: (1) identification for special education (also called eligibility); (2) educational placement (once identified as eligible for special education); and (3) discipline.

Social Justice

This term represents both an awareness of how social privilege and oppression impact school environments and the courage to contend with these complicated societal ills. School counselors can foster social justice with an awareness of inequity and a willingness to advocate for minoritized communities.

Social Stratification

Heard-Garris et al. (2018) contend that social stratification fosters prejudice, violence, and negative and harmful beliefs about racial outgroups – historically excluded racial groups of people with whom someone does not identify in their social strata – by both individuals and social institutions. Similarly, social stratification influences children's social-emotional identity development, particularly for Black, Latine, Asian, Native American, and Indigenous children and families challenged by economic vulnerability. Ultimately, the interplay between *social position*, racism, and segregation creates unique hierarchical barriers in American society. Their development often occurs in the face of structural barriers that are intentional and undergirded by a social disregard for their lives and emotional well-being.

Tribal Colleges and Universities (TCUs)

The establishment of the first Tribal college was on a remote reservation of the Navajo Nation. There are currently 35 TCUs across the United States, mainly in the Midwest and Southwest regions. Despite TCU's foundation beginning in the 1960s, it was not until 1994 that the federal government granted TCUs land grant status.

School Counseling Clinical and Skills-Related Terminology

Career Counseling

An aspect of education that involves school counselors engaging in conversations with students and parent/guardian/caretakers about interests leading to potential future occupations for students. Career counseling can begin at any grade level.

Classroom or Large Group Counseling

A role school counselors use to meet with many students within a classroom or auditorium setting to deliver a curriculum, a special activity, or an assembly. Such counseling can often be a daunting experience for novice and seasoned school counselors alike. These environments can be unpredictable and often require additional support that may not be available. These events have the potential for discipline issues to emerge. Preplanning for potential obstacles is necessary.

Culturally Responsive and Sustainable Application

School counselors get involved in many different activities and have a wide influence on students, staff, and families. Culture and context must be examined when planning, developing, and delivering services (Betters-Bubon et al., 2016). Responding to the demographics, cultural traditions, and strengths of the school and community can offer new and innovative ways that go beyond simply providing programs that are one-time initiatives. School counselors can be transformative.

Individual Counseling

One or more encounters whereby the school counselors meet with a student, parent/guardian/caretaker, teacher, or others in the school community on an individual basis to discuss a wide range of topics and issues. School counselors even work with children as young as four years old; however, skills beyond talk therapy will be needed for this unique population of youth.

Small Group Counseling

This role involves a school counselor facilitating dialog among two or more students working on a shared task(s) and developing supportive relationships. Small groups can be facilitated using a virtual platform. Small groups can be used as an intervention and also for data collection. As scholars call for student's voices to be included in educational reform efforts, group counseling offers a platform for such engagement (Ieva et al., 2022). Such action-oriented groups answer important questions that policymakers might not be addressing.

School Counseling Collaboration and Partnership-Related Terminology

Family Engagement

This term represents two-way, strengths-based collaboration among schools and families to foster growth for children, staff, and families alike (Halgunseth et al., 2009; Melzi et al., 2020; Posey-Maddox, 2017). This approach often centers on proactive communication, extending learning through home-school connections, and building relationships between school professionals and families in their local communities. Such collaboration is distinct from conventional parent involvement, which often creates barriers to full participation and focuses on what parents are *doing* in school to serve the needs of the privileged few. Meaningful family engagement often challenges inequitable power relations via expectations, beliefs, and norms for practices with historically excluded staff and parents.

Juneteenth

A federal holiday in the United States commemorating the emancipation of enslaved African Americans. Juneteenth marks the anniversary of the announcement from a famous commanding officer on June 19, 1865, proclaiming freedom for slaves in Galveston, Texas. Schools can more easily celebrate this holiday, yet will need to be intentional about finding creative ways to celebrate the accomplishments of Black people across the notoriety spectrum. It can be an opportunity to learn and appreciate more untold stories of members of the Black community.

Mental Health

Indicator or way of living that includes our emotional, psychological, and social well-being and their impacts on thoughts, feelings, and actions. Black and Brown students and families may have different experiences and/or perceptions of mental health. School counselors can confirm, support, or contradict these held beliefs.

Parent Liaison

A school support staff professional who links families to several resources needed to ensure students can focus on academic, social, emotional, and career development (Grant & Ray, 2019; Sanders, 2008). Parent liaisons will often have personal experiences with the schools as current or former parents in the school or district. A parent liaison is hired by the central office to work in one or more schools; thus, their roles vary across many dimensions. School counselors would benefit from knowing the parent liaison or the individual who would take on a similar role.

Parent Teacher Association (PTA)

An organization devoted to furthering the safety and interests of children and families in schools across the nation. The PTA can have a negative or positive connotation depending on how well they help families feel included, heard, and seen. In a school setting, a school counselor may be viewed as a key asset to the PTA, but it is often the school counselor who would need to make the effort to connect with the PTA. The obvious reason would be to work collaboratively; however, playing an advocacy role as a school counselor (i.e., staff PTA member) could cause some tension. For instance, you may attend a meeting and hear information that contradicts what you might be seeing or experiencing within the school regularly. Being aware of opportunities that arise to address inequities is important. Being brave enough to speak up and address these inequities is quite difficult if there are long-standing traditions that work to maintain these inequities.

Watch Dads of Great Students (D.O.G.S.)

A school-based program that aims to provide an avenue for fathers, male guardians, and male caregivers to serve as a liaison connecting schools and communities/families. This engaging program is gendered based on the terminology, however, non-traditional fathers as well as those who identify across the gender spectrum are welcomed as individual families determine their "father figures" (e.g., uncles, older cousins, etc). This program is available across school levels but is most commonly found in elementary and middle schools.

School Counseling Culture and Climate-Related Terminology

Anti-Blackness

The tenacious and relentless imagined narrative about Black people that shapes the experiences they often encounter within educational contexts. This inequity can be summed up as Black children having never really been given an equitable opportunity to succeed in schools (Williams & Graham,

2020). Yet many are resilient and overcome these institutional barriers. School counselors can help Black students by honestly and openly drawing attention to barriers that could be disguised as school mandates, policies, or historical precedence. Asking tough questions can help shine a light on unspoken rules, such as taking a certain number of racially minoritized students in honors classes. Once this type of barrier is removed, the brilliance of Black students and families can more freely emerge.

Anti-Black Racism

This term represents (a) historic oppression and unequal inclusion in the political, societal, and economic fabric of the United States; (b) pernicious stereotypes that essentialize and stigmatize Black people as a racial group; (c) legal precedence, policy, several barriers that systematically stifle educational and social mobility for Black individuals; and (d) ideology that justifies the domination and oppression of Black people (Sawyer, 2008). Roysicar and colleagues offer concrete examples of anti-Black racism within different aspects of society (e.g., health care, education, sports, child welfare, and voting rights). These authors also provide strategies that include less emphasis on deficits and more concerted efforts at celebrating the strengths and attributes of Black students. To illustrate, school counselors can create programs that affirm Black culture. School counselors can also challenge the administration team to not compare Black students with other groups, especially White students. When this comparison is eliminated and appropriate support is provided, racism towards Black people is interrupted.

Antiracism

An action-oriented concept coined by Ibram Kendi in his seminal book How to Be an Antiracist (2019). It is a conscious and deliberate effort to confront the impact and perpetuation of institutional White racial power, presence, and privilege as often as possible. Within a school setting, Antiracist efforts may come from individuals or small groups of individuals coming together to address any issue students are facing. It is important to note that an *Antiracist* is someone who actively fights racism and its effects wherever they may exist (Singleton, n.d.). This person can fight inequities by highlighting and promoting the brilliance and strengths within the cultures for which they are advocating. School counselors from all races can be Antiracists. Holcomb-McCoy (2022) offers a body of work featuring the extraordinary commitment of champions fighting racism even within themselves. The battlefields include both schools and communities. The professionals engaging in this work include counselors, mental health practitioners, educators, and researchers.

Blackness

An acknowledgment, acceptance, appreciation, and intentional view of Black people, Black culture, and anything associated with the Black population as a strength of students (Steen et al., 2023). School counselors may hear more commonly used terms like Afrocentric or Afrocentrism, which take a view of centering the history of people of African descent. Blackness is an inclusive term, and Afrocentrism is the foundation upon which Blackness is built. These terms can be used interchangeably. It can be assumed that these terms are appropriate or acceptable; however, members of your school community – particularly the members who are Black themselves – should get to weigh in on what would be the more appropriate terminology.

Discrimination

The unjust or prejudicial treatment of different categories of people or things, especially on the grounds of race, age, or sex. Both privileged and racial/ethnic minoritized populations are capable of discrimination; however, systemic discrimination is often only possible with those holding the most power. In a school setting, discrimination can be seen within many contexts, but special education is particularly salient.

Whiteness

This term has been understood most recently as centralizing power, status, and identity associated with racial hierarchy. In the past, Whiteness was intentionally used by the higher class to retain power by providing a psychological wage linked to social gain for White employees (Allen, 1994; DuBois, 1998). According to Bayne and colleagues, "Whiteness concepts are thus varied, with different vantage points of how White people might engage in the consideration of power, privilege, and racism, and what potential implications these constructs might have on their development" (p. 14, 2021). Counseling psychologist Janet Helms created a White racial identity development model that requires a conscious decision by the White individual to end any visible racism that may be within one's reach (Helms, 2020).

Additional terminology that may be useful within a school setting could include but not be limited to social class, educational level, privilege, oppression, and microaggressions. These concepts and ideas can be found within many different sources and are important frameworks to consider. According to Graham and Harris (2013), some mental health and school professionals make assumptions about children and adolescents based on their racial and ethnic backgrounds and their family's socioeconomic status. Having a deeper understanding of these terms while exploring one's own identity can provide areas for self-growth and better perspective-taking. Embracing these terms and concepts will influence your school counseling philosophy. We are hopeful that the authors' own personal and professional experiences will help the reader find ways to explore their own lives in understanding these complex topics.

School Counseling Tasks and Roles: Related Terminology

Consultation

A role that school counselors fulfill by making a connection with any number of school partners to explore ideas, suggestions, and strategies to address a particular concern that involves the consultee or others within the school community. As a consultant, a school counselor can make far-reaching impacts.

Coordination

A way that school counselors make connections between the resources available within the school and extended communities and the members of the school community. Coordination can maximize a school counselor's reach.

Program Evaluation

A skill that school counselors develop that includes a regular and routine system for collecting, analyzing, and using data to examine what is working and how well it is working, with an understanding of continuous program advancement for any organized school-related event(s), action(s), and/or intervention(s). School counselors can use available resources to evaluate their programs. School counselors can also be creative and develop relevant materials to evaluate the different programs, especially because many of the traditional evaluation tools were developed mainly on the perspective and experiences of White students, and White males in particular.

Student Scheduling

An administrative task that middle and high school counselors do in order to periodically create class assignments for students throughout the school year. This activity can be done by school counselors for students at nearly any time. It is important to know that this task is very time-consuming. When a student is moved from one class to another it is also potentially disruptive to the teachers and other students in several ways. For example, students' seating arrangements may need to be altered or a team of students may have to adjust to a new member. A student transferring from one class to another may need to adjust to a different curriculum, which can be a hardship for both the student and the teacher.

Student Registration

An administrative task that some school counselors conduct to ensure new or transferring students are placed in the appropriate grade levels, receive the correct number of transferable credits (if applicable), and have a solid plan for matriculation through the current school and school district. Registering students is not an easy endeavor. Students transferring from other districts, even those outside of the US, may have taken classes that do not easily translate into the current district's program of studies (i.e., curriculum). School counselors will use negotiation and investigative skills to provide the most appropriate placement for students. Advocacy is ensuring that technicalities do not prevent students from successfully matriculating through the system.

Definition Activity

The definitions for the 504 Plan and Individualized Education Program are provided in the full Key Terms section earlier in the chapter. In addition to reviewing these definitions, we ask you to apply your understanding of these definitions and come up with two or three scenarios where you have seen or experienced discrimination. Following these scenarios, take a moment to consider what is important to you through reflection questions.

Reflection Questions

1 What were the racial and cultural makeups of the students, families, faculty, and staff in your scenario?
2 If you were to use other examples of racial and cultural factors, then how would this change the imagined outcome?
3 What draws your energy or compels you to draw attention to this essential belief or passion?
4 What would you do without this, and how are you passing this idea to others?
5 Thinking about the "why" is critical and can help develop a lifestyle and strategy in a school counseling context that will work long-term.

School Counseling Philosophy

What is needed to be a thoughtful, impactful, engaged practitioner-scholar who is committed and willing to stretch and grow? It is time for the school counseling profession to include the question "Why do we engage in this work?" (Chris Sink, personal communication). This question will help motivate our efforts and shed light on sustainability and prevent burnout. The level of commitment required to be a school counselor cannot be overstated; however, not all school counselors experience burnout despite their tireless efforts. Understanding the why behind the fight for equity and justice within school settings can help develop a sustainable school counseling philosophy.

The role(s) of the school counselor is often outlined within professional organizations and counselor education programs. The American School Counselor Association (ASCA), through the ASCA National Model and other influential documents (ASCA, 2016), clearly defines actions for the contemporary school counselor. These actions are important; however, developing an internal, personal, and connected view of one's philosophical underpinnings can offer a clear motivation for actively engaging in these daunting efforts.

Cultural Responsiveness, Sustainability, and Application

We use the terms culturally responsive and culturally sustainable interchangeably. Further, there are numerous ways to describe cultural responsiveness or sustainability, but, instead, we emphasize actions and applications that nourish strengths within communities in culturally appropriate ways. It is necessary to apply race and culture in ways that reflect a conscious effort in creating programs, evaluations, and lessons that are inclusive and reflective of the potential of students and families. Examining these activities at this stage in a school counselor's identity development can shed light on what cultural applications could be implemented within a school setting.

For this activity, three examples are provided for consideration of what might align with your current understanding of your school counseling philosophy. Reflect and compare the two versions provided. Consider how these three examples can be more culturally appropriate, based on a school within your local community.

Example 1

The first example is a preview of a high school counselor's *Calendar of Events*. Brainstorm the emerging details of these events below:

2021 – 2022 Mystery High School (MHS) EVENTS
(assumes in-person unless noted)

8/24: College Jump Start Noon – 3:00 p.m. library
9/15: Senior Parent Night, in person and live streamed
9/23: Junior Parent Coffee – Naviance – virtual
9/23: 1st Senior Breakfast & Meeting – library and auditorium
10/6: Fin Aid Night – virtual with Ignite High and Badger High
10/13: FAFSA Complete night – virtual with Ignite High and Badger High
10/23: Practice SAT – in person – library 8:00 a.m. to Noon
12/3: Teacher Scholarship Fundraiser Auction virtual & in person in Career Center
12/7: Junior Night – in person and live stream
12/9: ASVAB test – Career Center
12/14: 2nd Senior Breakfast & Meeting – library and auditorium
1/6: Rising 9th Curriculum Night and current 9th–11th Grade Curriculum Night
1/13: Parent Coffee for Juniors – Fin Aid – virtual
2/24: 3rd Senior Break and Meeting – library and auditorium
2/24: ELL Night – virtual
3/14: Job Fair – hosted by MHS (invited SJHS, IHS, SBJH, FHJH & BBHS) in person – need Main Gym. If not available, we need a new night with Main Gym. The cafeteria does not work.
4/20: Current Freshmen and Sophomores Night – Auditorium
4/22: Parent Coffee for Freshmen parents – what they should be doing & Naviance
5/6: Decision Day & 4th Quarter Breakfast – library and main gym
6/8: Senior Awards & Gala (pending ACL graduation dates)
6/9: All School Awards – THIS SHOULD BE VIRTUAL
TBD Events
4 Colleges You Should Know – TBD April
Spring Junior Panel – TBD – hosted by another high school

Example 1 Discussion Questions

1 What stands out to you at this point?
2 Choose a date and an event. What specifically could you create regarding this event?
3 Describe the students you hope to serve. How would you modify your events if delivering them in an elementary school setting to ensure they are developmentally appropriate and inclusive?

Example 2

The second example is a short evaluation tool that could be used in a middle school setting. Review the SMART Goals pre- and post-assessment that could be used to gauge what middle school students understand about goal setting.

SMART Goals pre and post

For each of the following statements, indicate the extent to which you agree or disagree (Table 1.1).

Table 1.1 SMART Goals (Pre- and Post-Assessment)

	Strongly Agree	Somewhat Agree	Neutral	Somewhat Disagree	Strongly Disagree	Don't Know
1) I know how to define goal setting.	(5)	(4)	(3)	(2)	(1)	(0)
2) I plan to set personal goals in school.	(5)	(4)	(3)	(2)	(1)	(0)
3) I plan to set academic goals in school.	(5)	(4)	(3)	(2)	(1)	(0)
4) I know what a SMART goal means.	(5)	(4)	(3)	(2)	(1)	(0)
5) I use SMART goals when I plan.	(5)	(4)	(3)	(2)	(1)	(0)

Example 2 Discussion Questions Part 1

1   Based on your school counseling philosophy, does this tool reflect your student population? If so, what indicators confirm that students will see themselves in this assessment?
2   If this tool does not reflect your student population, then what language could be infused within this tool to ensure inclusivity? There are numerous ways to modify the language to align with your school counseling philosophy. For example, a school counselor might write, "Dear students, look at these questions and be as honest as you can. Mark the number that matches how you feel about the question and what you believe the answer is. Feel free to write notes or questions you have about this survey in the last column marked 'question/comments.'" (Table 1.2)

Table 1.2 SMART Goals (Planning with Students)

	Yes	Somewhat or Maybe	Not Sure	Not Really	No	Question/ Comments
1) I know how to explain goal setting to my friends and family.	(5)	(4)	(3)	(2)	(1)	
2) I plan to set goals in school that both I and my family would be proud of.	(5)	(4)	(3)	(2)	(1)	
3) I plan to set goals that will help me have a better future after I graduate from school.	(5)	(4)	(3)	(2)	(1)	
4) I can explain SMART goals to my friends and family.	(5)	(4)	(3)	(2)	(1)	
5) I will use SMART goals when I make goals in the future.	(5)	(4)	(3)	(2)	(1)	

Example 2 Discussion Questions Part 2

1 What do you think about the way this assessment was modified?
2 How did it differ from or align with your own example?
3 What is your key takeaway from adjusting this tool?

Example 3

The third example is a set of short scenarios for elementary students that are part of a classroom lesson. The following short scenarios are part of an elementary school counseling lesson titled "Being Proactive" – a topic that encourages responsible action. The short scenarios can be used to explore social skills (Table 1.3).

Example 3 Discussion Questions

1 When reviewing the scenarios above, what changes would you make?
2 Would you change the language (e.g., words used) or the content? For example, how could you approach the choices in names?
3 From a broader perspective, what could you do to ensure your curriculum materials are culturally sustaining?
4 If there are barriers, how might they be overcome?

Table 1.3 Scenarios for "Being Proactive" Exercise with Students

Mark was a new student at school. He walked in with a smile and introduced himself to his classmates.	Tracy was at her sister's volleyball game. She was bored and sat on the bench looking around for hours.
Rick was assigned a project on Mercury. He didn't know anything about Mercury but was willing to research and learn about it.	Amanda got frustrated with her homework and crumpled the paper into a ball.
Misty missed her friends from her old school so she decided to call them and set up a time together.	Sarah and Lacey were fighting for a spot in line. Sarah elbowed Lacey out of the way to get ahead of her.
Susan was running an errand for her teacher and the halls were empty. She walked quietly to the office to drop off the important note and walked back.	Jason was playing football during recess. He dropped the ball and lost the point. He yelled at his teammates for not playing well.

Summary

In summary, making cultural applications is a choice. Scholars have long argued that preservice school counselors (counselors in training) need to understand that their roles will continue to evolve and change throughout their professional careers. Brott and Myers (1999), suggested that school counselors will ultimately make choices that determine the counseling program and services offered in their school. In other words, apart from school principals and school counseling directors, school counselors essentially have the freedom to implement programs that align with their philosophy. The more comfortable they are with taking action, the more influential their activities. A seminal study found that the development of school counselors consisted of becoming increasingly aware of the differences between what they had learned in their training programs and the realities of the field (Brott & Myers, 1999). It was assumed they either adjusted to what was presented daily or decided to leave the field. The current political climate will make functioning with more freedom daunting, especially when taking a stance on equity. Skills are needed to broach race and culture toward equity in schools. It will be imperative to overcome fear and recognize that the fight for liberation is done collectively.

Key Takeaways

1 Education is not equal for all students.
2 "Being a school counselor comes with the privilege and duty to encourage change talk regarding racism."

3   Systemic racism is still present in our society and impacts our schools, but school counselors can engage in a fight for equity for all.

Chapter Application

1   Examine your current understanding of your school counseling philosophy. What are identifiable strengths that will help you to adhere to this philosophy? What are areas of growth needed to fulfill this philosophy? To what extent are you able to see the impact of your racial and cultural identities?

2   Critically reflect on this note from Sam's narrative. He wrote, "I wondered if my educational experiences might have been quite different had I been educated in Mississippi." What if you were a Black male and were educated within the state in which you live? What might your experiences be like? If you are a Black male, what was your experience like? How does this information influence the actions and behaviors you will take over the course of your career?

3   You accept a job at a school in which the students are primarily Black and Brown; however, not all of the students are from minoritized backgrounds. Explore your own intersections of identity in relation to student populations that you feel most comfortable working with and those identities you feel less comfortable working with. Explore reactions you may have when working with these students and strategies for alleviating these concerns. Who may be more likely to experience some form of discrimination or oppression even in school? What activities will you use to connect students, families, faculty members, and staff members to advocate with and on behalf of minoritized populations in your school?

Reference

Allen, T. (1994). *The invention of the White race*. Verso.

American School Counselor Association (ASCA). (2016). ASCA ethical standards for school counselors. *ASCA*. https://www.schoolcounselor.org/asca/media/asca/Ethics/EthicalStandards2016.pdf

Baker, S. B., & Gerler, E. R. (2008). *School counseling for the twenty-first century* (5th ed.). Upper Saddle River, NJ: Pearson/Merrill.

Betters-Bubon, J., Brunner, T., & Kansteiner, A. (2016). Success for all? The role of the school counselor in creating and sustaining culturally responsive positive behavior interventions and supports programs. *Professional Counselor, 6*(3), 263–277.

Brott, P. E., & Myers, J. E. (1999). Development of a professional school counselor identity: A grounded theory. *Professional School Counseling, 2*(5), 339–348.

Cole, K., & Verwayne, D. (2018). Becoming upended: Teaching and learning about race and racism with young children and their families. *Young Children, 73*(2), 34–43. https://www.naeyc.org/resources/pubs/yc/may2018/teaching-learning-race-and-racism

Crenshaw, K. (1991). Mapping the margins: Intersectionality, identity politics, and violence against women of color. *Stanford Law Review, 43*(6), 1241. 10.2307/1229039.

Day-Vines, N. L., Bryan, J., & Griffin, D. (2013). The Broaching attitudes and behavior survey (BABS): An exploratory assessment of its dimensionality. *Journal of Multicultural Counseling and Development, 41*(4), 210–223. 10.1002/j.2161-1912.2013.00037.x

Day-Vines, N. L., Bryan, J., Brodar, J. R., & Griffin, D. (2021). Grappling with race: A national study of the broaching attitudes and behavior of school counselors, clinical mental health counselors, and counselor trainees. *Journal of Multicultural Counseling and Development, 50*(1), 25–34. 10.1002/jmcd.12231

DuBois, W. E. B. (1998). *Black reconstruction in America 1860–1880.* New York, NY: Free Press. (Original work published 1935)

Graham, J. A., & Harris, Y. R. (2013). Children of color and parental incarceration: Implications for research, theory, and practice. *Journal of Multicultural Counseling and Development, 41*(2), 66–81. 10.1002/j.2161-1912.2013.00028.x

Grant, K. B., & Ray, J. A. (2019). *Home, school, and community collaboration: Culturally responsive family engagement* (4th ed.). Washington, DC: SAGE. ISBN: 9781506365732

Halgunseth, L., Peterson, A. , & Moodie, S. (2009). Family engagement, diverse families, and early childhood education programs: An integrated review of the literature. *Young Children, 64*(5), 56–58.

Heard-Garris, N.J., Cale, M., Camaj, L., Hamati, M.C., & Dominguez, T.P. (2018). Transmitting trauma: A systematic review of various racism and child health. *Social Science & Medicine, 199*, 230–240. 10.1016/j.socscimed.2017.04.018

Helms, J. E. (2020). *A race is a nice thing to have: A guide to being a white person or understanding the white persons in your life.* Cognella.

Holcomb-McCoy, C. (February, 2022). *School counseling to close opportunity gaps: A social justice and antiracist framework for success* (2nd ed.). Thousand Oaks, CA: Corwin. [Foreword by Dr. Ibram X Kendi].

Hughes, D., & Chen, L. (1997) When and what parents tell children about race: An examination of race-related socialization among African American families. *Applied Developmental Science, 1*(4), 200–214. 10.1207/s1532480xads0104_4

Ieva, K. P., Steen, S., & Beasley, J. J. (2022). Preparing school counselors for social justice group counseling: Examining, power, privilege, and intersectionality. *Counselor Education and Supervision.*

James, A., Coard, S., Fine, M., & Rudy, D. (2018). The central roles of race and racism in reframing family systems theory: A consideration of choice and time. *Journal of Family Theory and Review, 10*(2), 419–433. 10.1111/jftr.12262

Melzi, G., McWayne, C., & Ochoa, W. (2020). Family engagement and Latine children's early narrative skills. *Early Childhood Education Journal, 50*, 83–95. 10.1007/s10643-020-01132-7

Posey-Maddox, L. (2017). Schooling in suburbia: The intersections of race, class, gender, and place in black fathers' engagement and family–school relationships. *Gender and Education, 5,* 577–593. 10.1080/09540253.2016.1274389

Sanders, M. G. (2008). How parent liaisons can help bridge the home-school gap. *The Journal of Educational Research, 101*(5), 287–298. 10.3200/JOER.101.5. 287-298

Sawyer, M. Q. (2008). DuBois's double consciousness versus Latin American exceptionalism: Joe Arroyo, Salsa, and Négritude. In M. Marable and V. Agard-Jones (Eds.), *Transnational black-ness: Navigating the global color line* (pp. 135–148). Palgrave MacMillan.

Spencer, M. B., Dupree, D., Tinsley, B., McGee, E., Hall, J., Fegley, S., Elmore, T., Graham, S., Urdan, T., McCormick, C., Harris, K., Sweller, J., & Sinatra, G. (2011). Resistance and resiliency in a color-conscious society: Implications for learning and teaching. In K. R. Harris, S. Graham, and T. Urdan (Eds.), *APA educational psychology handbook, Vol 1: Theories, constructs, and critical issues* (pp. 461–494). American Psychological Association. 10.1037/13273-016

Steen, S., Vannatta, R., & Ieva, K. P. (2023). *Introduction to group counseling: A culturally sustaining and inclusive framework.* New York, NY: Springer Publishing.

Steen, S., Bethea, C., & Davis, J. L. (2023). Reconceptualizing the achieving success everyday group counseling model to focus on the needs of black male middle school youth. *Journal of School-Based Counseling Policy and Evaluation, 5*(1), 4–20.

Strategies for Broaching the Subjects of Race, Ethnicity, and Culture. Available from: https://www.researchgate.net/publication/352278937_Strategies_for_Broaching_the_Subjects_of_Race_Ethnicity_and_Culture [accessed Sep 05 2022].

Studer, J. R. (2015). *The essential school counselor in a changing society.* Thousand Oaks, CA: SAGE. https://doi.org/10.4135/9781483399881

Swanson, D., Spencer, M., Harpalani, V., Dupree, D., Noll, E., Ginzburg, S., & Seaton, G. (2003). Psychosocial development in racially and ethnically diverse youth: Conceptual and methodological challenges in the 21st century. *Development and Psychopathology, 15*(3), 743–771. 10.1017/S0954579403000361

Williams, S. M., & Graham, J. (2020). Cross-racial interactions in schools 65 years after Brown. *Peabody Journal of Education, 94*(5), 545–554. 10.1080/0161956X. 2019.1668211

Chapter 2

Identity Development of Racial/ Ethnic Minoritized Children

Key Terms (See Chapter 1)
Race, Racial identity, Racial identity development, Racial socialization

Author Narrative: Amber Sansbury

When I think of my racial identity development, the context stems from my family story. I grew up in a loving household with three daughters in suburban Columbus, Georgia, surrounded by our warm grandparents, extended family, and church community. Weekends spent with our village filled us with laughter, joy, southern cooking, and good values to keep us grounded.

In retrospect, my parent's decision to live on the North side of town – which was known for schools of better quality and consisted of predominantly White residents, like in many American cities – was complex. My mom later shared with me that this choice brought trade-offs. For example, my sisters and I never missed out on opportunities to learn and grow. Our schools and surrounding neighborhood offered enrichment like sports, travel, libraries, clubs, music lessons, and leadership experiences. We were among the few Black students in our classes. I increasingly felt racially isolated in school. I was considered a typical nerdy, awkward kid who came alive in the classroom. I did not have the words for self-advocacy against slights when White peers sneered that I "acted smart." I knew that I *was* smart. I also knew that my cousins, who lived and went to school in South Columbus, were *also* smart. I was only beginning to process what it meant to be Black and my sense of place in and out of school.

Coded language steeped in negative racial attitudes went over my head until my earliest experience with racism in the third grade. My teacher was a middle-aged, austere, White woman with very low expectations of me. Week to week, she spent countless hours going over spelling and cursive handwriting. I loved writing in cursive! I would curl and loop my letters as

DOI: 10.4324/9781003226253-3

much as I could. One day, my teacher peered over my shoulder and groaned in the middle of class. "Why do you always write in cursive?" she asked. "I love it, and I'm good at it," I explained. Her smile turned into a pressed line while her face reddened. *"Who do you think you are?"*, she quipped. *"You* are not special, because you're good at writing in cursive." I will never forget how dejected I felt. As I have gotten older, I think back over that memory as my first experience with racism. I get angry. Not only did my peers make me feel different, but this teacher communicated that I was unwelcome to be myself. I reflect on my tense relationship with her and believe that my Blackness influenced her expectations and regard for me.

Thankfully, this interaction and negative teacher-student relationship were a singular occurrence. I have enjoyed and thrived under skilled, caring teachers throughout my academic journey mostly situated in majority White spaces. I graduated ninth in my class in a magnet high school, earned several college scholarships, and have been mentored well over the years. Both the maternal and paternal sides of my Black family consist of folks who have earned master's and doctoral degrees in various fields to guide me along the way. I do not take this support as an effect of Black social mobility for granted. I learned how to lean on family, friends, and school classmates to navigate the harsh realities as a Black student in stressful racialized situations – namely the vacillating low and high expectations, power-laden friendships, microaggressions, and daily stressors on my identity that compounded over time. Today, I am more aware of distinctions and similar experiences that many Black students have, based on contextual factors (e.g., achievement level, income, family background, ability level, immigration status, gender expression, sexual orientation, ethnicity, or physical features). As an educator and emerging researcher, I now strive to ensure that all children, personnel, and families can be free of racial barriers and be full participants in our schools.

Content

School counseling professionals must possess knowledge of developmental theory to cultivate a strong self-concept with students. Several key frameworks underpin counseling practices that promote a positive personal identity within students. Students learning, relationships, and lives cannot be separated from their culture and, indeed, are imbued with cultural dimensions that shape their growth within varying and overlapping contexts (Harkness et al., 2020; Harkness & Super, 2020; Liu et al., 2020; Tsamaase et al., 2020). As one major concept, the Developmental Niche consists of three primary elements of child development: a) social and physical settings; b) customs for raising children and parenting; and c) parent, family, or caregiver psychology toward children (Super & Harkness, 1986). These three components interact and converge with external systems (e.g., health, education, or social systems) to form the broad context of child development. A student's family relationships and interactions with peers and adults also shape their view of themselves (Super & Harkness, 1986, p. 552; Spencer et al., 2011). This understanding, along with inherent values and beliefs about developmental theories related to personal identity, must inform how school counselors understand their role in child development across various settings. School counselors ultimately play a critical part as ecological agents who are instrumental in setting the tone to foster conducive to school cultures, norms, and therapeutic approaches that scaffold students' identities.

Secondly, school counselors cannot ignore the role of social rank, segregation, and racism when discussing development. These issues fundamentally shape how we perceive and support children in America. For instance, *Who is innocent, smart, healthy, and capable of a range of human emotions, abilities, and behaviors?* Unfortunately, our perceptions and beliefs can fall along racial lines for Black and Brown students in particular (James et al., 2018). Failing to name and challenge racism, a silent culprit in American society broadly, and school systems in this context, reifies educational policies, procedures, and practices that impede child development. García Coll et al. (1996), nearly three decades ago, centered elements of social stratification as they prioritized the development of Black, Asian, Latine, multiracial, and Native American and Indigenous students.

These researchers established the Integrative Model for the Study of Developmental Competencies in Minority Children to reflect societal factors that encompass life for many students experiencing poverty and who hold racially and ethnically vulnerable backgrounds. Initially, this model (e.g., Integrative Model for the Study of Developmental Competencies in Minority Children, García Coll et al., 1996) defined social stratification as a hierarchical system that ranks or assigns value to persons based on socially-constructed demographic characteristics (i.e., social class, ethnicity, ability, and race). This responsive framework has been updated and continues to offer a lens through which school counselors can peel back the layers of personal identity while recognizing a range of student-lived experiences, perspectives, and interconnected behavioral and developmental processes (Marks et al., 2007). In a recent study, some children from various racial/ethnic backgrounds (e.g., Cambodian, Dominican, and Portuguese) reported having a strong ethnic pride and comfort level with those from similar backgrounds while also being comfortable with members from other races. This finding was for students who were older than six but younger than twelve, suggesting that racial and ethnic pride may be important even for students who are in elementary school. The authors observe that segregation, racism, and prejudice derive from power differentials between people within this hierarchical system and that there are grave effects on child and youth well-being and developmental processes.

Racial Socialization

There are common racial socialization processes and messages that are helpful for Black children in particular. Doucet et al. (2018) distinguish racial socialization from ethnic socialization, as the latter relates to identity formation among people of shared national origin, culture, language, and history within and across racial backgrounds. This racial socialization may include family monitoring, social cues in and out of school settings, cultural traditions, or modeled behaviors that cultivate an affirming racial identity and problem-solving skills for students of in- and out-groups of dominant racial categories. Various intersecting ecological factors such as family structures; socioeconomic status; race (James et al., 2018; Pattillo, 2005); religion (Avent et al., 2015; Voisin et al., 2016); gender (Burnett et al., 2022; Butler et al., 2018; Leath et al., 2019); language, immigration status, and ethnic acculturation (Cabrera et al., 2013; Jones & Erving, 2015; Pope-Davis et al., 2000); and cognitive ability (Grantham & Ford, 2003; Joe & Davis, 2009) can function as adaptive or maladaptive influences for Black children, based on their place in school environments and society overall. For example, Black families with higher socioeconomic status often alter the frequency and quality of family racial socialization messages to respond to the shifting nature of navigating racially isolating and segregated schools. In these instances, Black students must be skilled in decoding and responding to blatant racial violence *and* less conspicuous manifestations such as lower academic expectations and racial slurs in school (Osborne et al., 2022; Thomas & Blackmon, 2015).

We have come to discover time and time again that the developmental influence of social injustice, for Black children in particular, is exacerbated by disproportionately harmful outcomes like exclusionary discipline, limited access to high-quality instruction in emotionally safe schools, and biased placement for special education services starting in the earliest grades (Meek et al., 2020). Deliberate attention to the sociocultural factors that shape social injustice across our school-home-community settings will strengthen policies, professional development, and responsive outcomes of school counseling (e.g., family-school-community relationships, pathways to resolving student conflict, and meaningful assessment of program goals).

Hughes and Chen (1997) prioritize key themes of racial socialization messages including *preparation for bias, promotion of mistrust,* and *cultural* or *racial pride* for their study of 4- to 14-year-old Black students and their families. *Cultural pride* includes the ways in which families communicate celebration and knowledge of Black history, ethnic heritage, and Afrocentric art forms and cultural norms (p. 202). *Cultural pride* and *preparation for bias* are the most common kinds of racial socialization messages, perhaps because Black families may feel most comfortable and pull from family experiences or available educational resources associated with these messages. Conversations related to the *promotion of mistrust*, for example, to survive in the face of police brutality, can be complicated. Nuanced messages that foster uncertainty leave room for miscommunication and misinterpretation on both sides (Blanchard et al., 2019). Families intrinsically grapple with the right balance of ensuring child safety and instilling a strong self-concept as students find their place in and out of racially isolating environments. Collectively, racial socialization messages can engender resilience, adaptation, and a student's skill to challenge racism in and out of school, for Black children in particular (Caughy et al., 2006; Hurd et al., 2012; Neblett et al., 2009; Neville et al., 2017; Pope-Davis et al., 2000; Stevenson, 2014). As school counselors, prioritizing Black students' emergent racial identity is fundamental as they observe and take in what it means to be Black in America (Loyd & Williams, 2017; Roopnarine et al., 2014; Spencer & Markstrom-Adams, 1990).

Without transformative action during this historic time, anti-Black racism can reinforce problematic staff-student interactions, family-school relationships, and toxic collegial interactions that engender marginalizing school experiences to the detriment of everyone. Even implicit biases may foster harmful assumptions, microaggressions, or cultural miscues in a school counseling setting (Tuttle & Haskins, 2017; Velsor & Orozco, 2007). We want to shine a light on the Engaging, Managing, and Bonding through Race (EMBRace, Anderson & Stevenson, 2016; Anderson et al., 2018) Initiative – a dynamic school counseling resource that allows school counselors to promote antiracism and social justice interactions. Anderson and Stevenson (2019) found that EmbRace has a positive impact on youth behaviors, stress reduction, and coping responses to trauma from discriminatory racial encounters. This initiative reflects exemplary school counseling services to address students' and families' race-related stressors and to strengthen emotional skills, academic performance, and racial identity processes in coordination with families' strengths.

Next, identity development for all students is unique. However, Black students who experience positive ethnic/racial socialization benefit by having positive racial identity development. The positivity comes from a myriad of sources, and highlighted below is the impact of Black families.

Black families impact students' racial and academic development by:

- Promoting positive racial and ethnic socialization;
- Offering affirming peer networks;
- Creating emotionally supportive home environments with meaningful dialog with their children;
- Helping with homework; and
- Communicating clear behavioral limits.

Some barriers have been commonly found in school settings. One area directly related to race and culture is the extent to which students and teachers share these commonalities.

Cultural Mismatch

Time and time again, the teaching force is reported as being mainly White and female. Recently, it has been reported that 44% of US schools have no racial/ethnic minority teachers on staff. Many students finish school without ever having had a racial/ethnic minority teacher. It seems inevitable that cultural mismatches could occur. Factors contributing to cultural mismatch include:

- Cultural misunderstandings;
- Low expectations by school staff;
- Disparity in resources; and
- Parenting styles in conflict with the demands and expectations of traditional schools.

It is important to acknowledge that Black/African American people have been told systematically and consistently that they are inferior and incapable of high academic achievement. However, this narrative must change, and teachers can help by not disparaging students' performance while they navigate hostile and violent environments. Some suggest that Black students' performance in school justifies this low expectation for success. The authors of this text argue that Black students, despite being directly or indirectly told that they cannot perform at high levels, achieve greatness. Black students are resilient.

Suggestions from Black teachers who provide some evidence for what could work when educating Black students (and all students from any racial background) include fostering:

- An ethic of caring;
- A belief in students and their communities;
- Inclusion of the student's culture to improve academic success; and
- The importance of education for political and economic success.

A direct benefit that stems from integrating Black student culture into their academic, social-emotional, and career development is to eliminate the need for some Black students to code-switch. Code-switching can be defined as adapting to the dominant cultural standards in specific settings as a means to protect one's self or appear "acceptable." Code-switching is a result of White, middle-class norms that have determined social acceptability in the United States.

For these reasons, school counselors must examine their own social rank, positionality, and past experiences – imbued with privilege or marginalization – to acknowledge the racialized, gendered, or ableist learning conditions in their schools. Such ongoing critical reflection is imperative to lead Black students, in particular, to responsive mental health and counseling supports that promote antiracism and positive racial identity development specifically in partnership with students, colleagues, families, and the dynamic communities where they are situated.

Reflection

Think, Talk, Do

Think

Take a moment to reflect on your earliest school memory. To what extent were you aware of your race and/or the racial makeup of those around you? To what extent were you aware of inequities and unfair advantages? What recollections do you have regarding the strengths and cultural contributions of various racial groups represented within your school?

Talk

After reflecting on these ideas, take a moment to talk to someone else about what you have been thinking about. Share with a partner from your class or a group of peers. What impact did race have on your experiences navigating public schools? If more feasible, share this information with someone you trust within your family. Talk about it to make meaning of these reflections. Consider identifying key areas of new insight that have been gained from reflecting and sharing your past school experiences and the racial contexts.

Do

As you begin to understand more clearly what this early recollection of your own race or the racial makeup of others means to you, make a decision to do something with this new understanding. Devise a plan of action (i.e., something you can do realistically and within your purview) that you will commit to by the time you complete the reading of this text. Even small steps (e.g., creating an outline of ideas, or a one-page conceptual paper) that highlight future ideas will produce dividends.

Summary

As noted in Chapter 1, *racial identity* refers to an evolving, dynamic process influencing how children recognize, interpret, and act upon their racial selves and others in and out of their racial group. As we share in this chapter, students who can identify, respond to, and challenge racism – through the protective decisions of their families, school personnel, and friends in and out of school environments – can establish salient and essential emotional skills as a part of their emergent racial identity (Spencer et al., 2011). The extent to which children and adolescents find confidence, support, and sense of self in their racial identity could be fostered within schools. School counselors can play a role in promoting inclusive spaces. However, this work must be intentional, and professionals would do well to have a personal understanding of what positive racial identity means for them in order to help children and adolescents explore and embrace their own.

Key Takeaways

1 It is necessary to reflect on your own racial and ethnic socialization in your family of origin and its impact on the counselor-student relationship.
2 Work to cultivate curiosity, openness, and knowledge about the racialized experiences of others that differ from your own.
3 School counselors have a role in fostering positive racial identity in students and creating an affirming school climate in partnership with students' families, colleagues, administrators, and their wider school community.
4 We need to build counseling strategies, models, and skills that enable school stakeholders to cope with and combat racism at their stage of personal and professional development.

Chapter Application

1 Apply takeaways to consider your role in collaborating with the student's classroom teachers and family as partners in racial identity development. Discuss relevant resources in small groups.
2 Reflect on the following as a group:

- What are common racial-ethnic socialization messages or themes with children in your life (e.g., in your life, school, or clinical practice)? Examples may include *preparation for bias, racial or cultural pride, egalitarianism, promotion of mistrust,* and *spirituality* or belief in one's dignity or higher calling.
- To what extent do these racial-ethnic socialization messages differ from what you heard or learned implicitly from your own family of origin growing up; i.e., your biological/adoptive/chosen parents, siblings, and yourself?
- Share your insights with a colleague or classmate. What did you learn from their racial-ethnic socialization message as a family? How might their experiences expand your view of parenting and racial-ethnic socialization within families?

3   As school counseling professionals, we must *think critically* and deliberately *plan* how we might support positive racial identity in partnership with school colleagues, families, and students. With this in mind, consider the following prompts as a group:

- What are the promotive roles and benefits of racial identity development? For students? Their parents and families?
- How can you become more equipped by strengthening your own racial identity development individually and with other school counselors?
- As a trained school counselor, how might you 1) deepen conversations about race and racism in your school 2) work to resolve racism-related conflicts in your school community 3) build on racial identity development as an asset for an affirming school climate?

Reference

Anderson, R. E., & Stevenson, H. C. (2016). EMBRace training manual. Unpublished training manual, Racial Empowerment Collaborative, Graduate School of Education, University of Pennsylvania.

Anderson, R. E., Jones, S. C. T., Navarro, C., McKenny, M., Mehta, T., & Stevenson, H. C. (2018). Addressing the mental health needs of Black American youth and families: A case study from the EMBRace intervention. *International Journal of Environmental Research and Public Health, 15,* 898. 10.3390/ijerph15050898

Anderson, R. E., & Stevenson, H. C. (2019). RECASTing racial stress and trauma: Theorizing the healing potential of racial socialization in families. *American Psychologist, 74*(1), 63–75. 10.1037/amp0000392

Avent, J., Cashwell, C., & Brown-Jeffy, S. (2015). African American pastors on mental health, coping, and help-seeking. *Counseling and Values, 60,* 32–47. 10.1002/j.2161-007x.2015.00059.x

Blanchard, S. B., Coard, S. I., Hardin, B. J., & Mereoiu, M. (2019). Use of parental racial socialization with African American toddler boys. *Journal of Child and Family Studies, 28*, 387–400. 10.1007/s10826-018-1274-2

Burnett, M., McBride, M. S., Green, M.N., Cooper, S. M. (2022). "When I think of Black girls, I think of opportunities": Black girls' identity development and the protective role of parental socialization in educational settings. *Frontiers in Psychology*, 13, 933476. 10.3389/fpsyg.2022.933476

Butler-Barnes, S. T., Leath, S., Williams, A., Byrd, C., Carter, R., Chavous, T. M. (2018). Promoting resilience among African American girls: Racial identity as a protective factor. *Child Development, 89*(6), e552–e571. 10.1111/cdev.12995

Cabrera, N., Beeghley, M., & Einsenberg, N. (2013). Positive development of minority children: Introduction to the special issue. *Social Policy Report, 27*(2), 1–30. 10.1111/j.1750-8606.2012.00253.x

Caughy, M., Nettles, S., O'Campo, P., & Lohrfink, M. (2006). Neighborhood matters: Racial socialization of African American children. *Child Development, 77*(5), 1220–1236. 10.1111/j.1467-8624.2006.00930.x

Doucet, F., Banerjee, M., & Parade, S. (2018). What should young Black children know about race? Parents of preschoolers, preparation for bias, and promoting egalitarianism. *Journal of Early Childhood Research, 16*(1), 65–79. 10.1177/14 76718X16630763

García Coll, C., Lamberty, G., Jenkins, R., McAdoo, H. Crnic, K., Wasik, B., & Garcia, H. (1996). An integrative model for the study of developmental competencies in minority children. *Child Development, 67*, 1891–1914. 10.1111/j.14 67-8624.1996.tb01834.x

Grantham, T., & Ford, D. (2003). Beyond self-concept and self-esteem: Racial identity and gifted African American students. *The High School Journal, 87*(1), 18–29. 10.1353/hsj.2003.0016

Harkness, S., & Super, C. (2020). Why understanding culture is essential for supporting children and families. *Applied Developmental Science, 25*(1), 14–25. 10.1080/10888691.2020.1789354

Harkness, S., Super, C., Bonichini, S., Bermudez, M., Mavridis, C., Schaik, S., Tomkunas, A., & Palacios, J. (2020). Parents, preschools, and the developmental niches of young children: A study in four Western cultures. *New Directions for Child & Adolescent Development, 2020*(170), 113–141. 10.1002/cad.20343

Hughes, D., & Chen, L. (1997) When and what parents tell children about race: An examination of race-related socialization among African American families. *Applied Developmental Science, 1*(4), 200–214. /10.1207/s1532480xads0104_4

Hurd, N., Sánchez, B., Zimmerman, M., & Caldwell, C. (2012). Natural mentors, racial identity, and educational attainment among African American adolescents: Exploring pathways to success. *Child Development, 83*(4), 1196–1212. 10.1111/j.1467-8624.2012.01769.x

James, A., Coard, S., Fine, M., & Rudy, D. (2018). The central roles of race and racism in reframing family systems theory: A consideration of choice and time. *Journal of Family Theory and Review, 10*(2), 419–433. 10.1111/jftr.12262

Joe, E., & Davis, J. (2009). Parental influence, school readiness and early academic achievement of African American boys (EJ878479). *The Journal of Negro Education, 78*(3), 260–276.

Jones, C., & Erving, C. (2015). Structural constraints and lived realities: Negotiating racial and ethnic identities for African Caribbeans in the United States. *Journal of Black Studies*, *46*(5), 521–546. 10.1177/0021934715586506

Leath, S., Mathews, C., Harrison, A., & Chavous, T. (2019). Racial identity, racial discrimination, and classroom engagement outcomes among Black girls and boys in predominately Black and predominantly white school districts. *American Educational Research Journal*, *56*(4), 1318–1352. 10.3102/0002831218816955

Liu, J., Harkness, S., & Harkness, C. (2020). Chinese mothers' cultural models of children's shyness: Ethnotheories and socialization strategies in the context of social change. *New Directions for Child & Adolescent Development*, *2020*(170), 69–92. 10.1002/cad.20340

Loyd, A., & Williams, B. (2017). The potential for youth programs to promote African American youth's development of ethnic and racial identity. *Child Development Perspectives*, *11*(1), 29–38. 10.1111/cdep.12204

Marks, A. K., Szalacha, L. A., Lamarre, M., Boyd, M. J., & García Coll, C. (2007). Emerging ethnic identity and interethnic group social preferences in middle childhood: Findings from the Children of Immigrants Development in Context (CIDC) study. *International Journal of Behavioral Development*, *31*(5), 501–513.

Meek, S., Iruka, I. U., Fernandez, V., Catherine, E., McIntosh, K., Gordon, L., Gilliam, W., Hemmeter, M. L., Blevins, D., & Powell, T. (2020). *Fourteen priorities to dismantle systemic racism in early care and education*. Tempe, AZ: Arizona State University, The Children's Equity Project.

Neblett, E., Smalls, C., Ford, K., Nguyen, H., & Sellers, R. (2009). Racial socialization and racial identity: African American parents' messages about race as precursors to identity. *Journal of Youth and Adolescence*, *38*(2), 189 203. 10.1007/s10964-008-9359-7

Neville, H., Cross, W., & Lee, R. (2017). Racial awakening: Epiphanies and encounters in Black racial identity. *Cultural Diversity and Ethnic Minority Psychology*, *23*(1), 102–108. 10.1037/cdp0000105

Osborne, K. R., Walsdorf, A. A., Smith-Bynum, M.A., Redig, S., Brinkley, D., Tresch Owen, M., O'Brien Caughy, M. (2022). Responding to racism at school: Ethnic-racial socialization and the academic engagement of Black and Latinx youth. *Child Development*, *000*, 1–18. 10.1111/cdev.13853

Pattillo, M. (2005). Black middle-class neighborhoods. *Annual Review of Sociology*, *31*, 305–329. 10.1146/annurev.soc.29.010202.095956

Pope-Davis, B., Liu, W., Ledesma-Jones, S., & Nevitt, J. (2000). African American acculturation and black racial identity: A preliminary investigation. *Journal of Multicultural Counseling and Development*, *28*(2), 98–112. doi:10.1002/j.2161-1912.2000.tb00610.x

Roopnarine, J., Krishnakumar, A., Narine, L., Logie, C., & Lape, M. (2014). Relationships between parenting practices and preschoolers' social skills in African, Indo, and mixed-ethnic families in Trinidad and Tobago: The mediating role of ethnic socialization. *Journal of Cross-Cultural Psychology*, *45*(3) 362–380. 10.1177/0022022113509884

Spencer, M. B., Dupree, D., Tinsley, B., McGee, E., Hall, J., Fegley, S., Elmore, T., Graham, S., Urdan, T., McCormick, C., Harris, K., Sweller, J., & Sinatra, G.

(2011). Resistance and resiliency in a color-conscious society: Implications for learning and teaching. In K. R. Harris, S. Graham, and T. Urdan (Eds.), *APA educational psychology handbook, Vol 1: Theories, constructs, and critical issues* (pp. 461–494). American Psychological Association. 10.1037/13273-016

Spencer, M. B., & Markstrom-Adams, C. (1990). Identity processes among racial and ethnic minority children in America. *Child Development, 61*(2), 290–310. 10.2307/1131095

Stevenson, H. (2014). *Promoting racial literacy in schools: Differences that make a difference.* Teachers College Press.

Super, C., & Harkness, S. (1986). The developmental niche: A conceptualization at the interface of child and culture. *International Journal of Behavioral Development, 9*(4), 545–569. 10.1177/016502548600900409

Tsamaase, M., Harkness, S., & Super, C. (2020). Grandmothers' developmental expectations for early childhood in Botswana. *New Directions for Child & Adolescent Development, 2020* (170), 93–112. 10.1002/cad.20335

Thomas, A. J. & Blackmon, S. M. (2015). The Influence of the Trayvon Martin shooting on racial socialization practices of African American parents. *Journal of Black Psychology, 41*(1) 75–89. 10.1177/0095798414563610

Tuttle, M., & Haskins, N. (2017). "A Different Way": The experiences of Latinx Parents with school counselors. *Journal for Social Action in Counseling & Psychology, 9*(2), 95–111. 10.33043/JSACP.9.2.95-111

Velsor, P. V. & Orozco, G. L. (2007). Involving low-income parents in the schools: Community centric strategies for school counselors. *Professional School Counseling, 11*(1), 17–24. 10.1177/2156759X070110

Voisin, D., Corbin, D., & Jones, C. (2016). A conceptualization of spirituality among African American young adults. *Western Journal of Black Studies, 40*(1), 14–23.

Chapter 3

The History of Education and Racial Disparities in Schools

Key Terms (See Chapter 1)
Social Justice, Black/Brown

Author Narrative: Shekila Melchior

When I began my career as a school counselor, I did not anticipate the experiences I would have. As a graduate of a Historically Black Institution, I found great value in being taught by educators who looked like me and by having a practicum and internship supervisor who also looked like me. The setting in which I interned was a low-income, majority-minority school in an urban area of a Southern state. My first school counselor position was in a low-income, majority-White, rural Southern state. Over the course of three years, I encountered both direct and indirect racism from students, their families, and school staff while advocating for more equitable treatment of my racial/ethnic minoritized students. I encountered significant roadblocks in my time at the school, and the issues of race and the historical systemic oppression from the county that I was in were pervasive. While I believed I served my students well, I would be remiss if I did not acknowledge the lack of preparation I felt.

Content

Defining Education and Educational Access

As shown in Figure 3.1, various historical, structural, and sociopolitical factors have shaped educational inequity for Black children in particular (Evans-Winters et al., 2018; Gilliam et al., 2016; González, 2004; Greenberg & Monarrez, 2019; Griffith et al., 2017; Iruka et al., 2021). Givens (2021) underscores the barriers and facilitators to child development before and after the pivotal *Brown v. Board of Education* (1954) Supreme Court decision.

DOI: 10.4324/9781003226253-4

Education History for Black Children & Youth in the U.S.

Key benchmarks and policy provisions

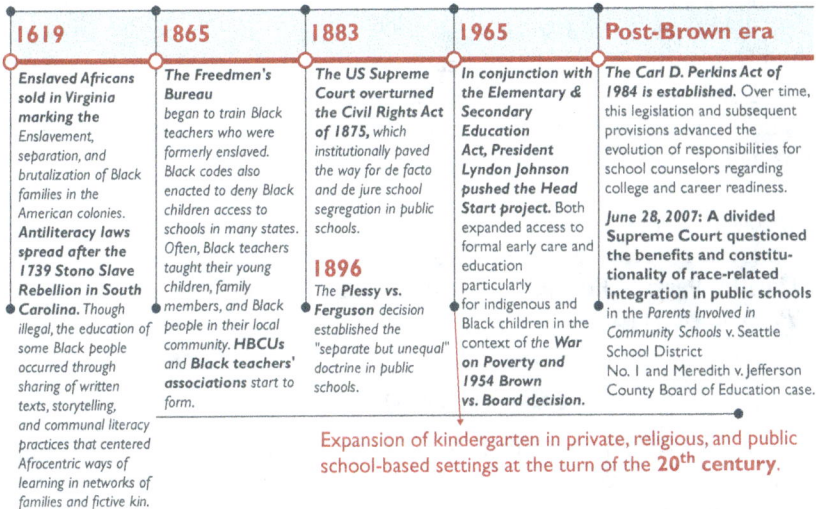

1619	1865	1883	1965	Post-Brown era
Enslaved Africans sold in Virginia marking the Enslavement, separation, and brutalization of Black families in the American colonies. **Antiliteracy laws** *spread after the 1739 Stono Slave Rebellion in South Carolina. Though illegal, the education of some Black people occurred through sharing of written texts, storytelling, and communal literacy practices that centered Afrocentric ways of learning in networks of families and fictive kin.*	*The Freedmen's Bureau began to train Black teachers who were formerly enslaved.* **Black codes** *also enacted to deny Black children access to schools in many states. Often, Black teachers taught their young children, family members, and Black people in their local community.* **HBCUs** *and* **Black teachers' associations** *start to form.*	*The US Supreme Court overturned the Civil Rights Act of 1875, which institutionally paved the way for de facto and de jure school segregation in public schools.* **1896** *The* **Plessy vs. Ferguson** *decision established the "separate but unequal" doctrine in public schools.*	*In conjunction with the Elementary & Secondary Education Act, President Lyndon Johnson pushed the Head Start project. Both expanded access to formal early care and education particularly for indigenous and Black children in the context of the War on Poverty and 1954 Brown vs. Board decision.*	*The Carl D. Perkins Act of 1984 is established.* Over time, this legislation and subsequent provisions advanced the evolution of responsibilities for school counselors regarding college and career readiness. June 28, 2007: A divided Supreme Court questioned the benefits and constitutionality of race-related integration in public schools in the *Parents Involved in Community Schools* v. Seattle School District No. 1 and Meredith v. Jefferson County Board of Education case.

Expansion of kindergarten in private, religious, and public school-based settings at the turn of the 20th century.

Figure 3.1 Timeline of historical benchmarks and policies influencing school counseling.

The onset of the Industrial Revolution brought growing numbers of European American children of affluent or moderately wealthy families into formal schooling (Herr, 2001). Though private tutors and public schools existed as valuable commodities, most of their African American, Latine, Asian, and Indigenous peers from lower-income households had limited access to adequate education because of legal school segregation and institutional barriers (Givens, 2021; Williams & Graham, 2020). Public schooling brought renewed public interest in child development and variables that influence students' well-being in and out of schools: violence, substance abuse, severe poverty, family structure and configuration, mental illness, and shifting marital patterns in the U.S. (Gysbers, 2001). Around the turn of the 20th century, wider early care and education access also presented a fundamental opportunity to redefine developmentally appropriate practices for preschool-aged children and families experiencing poverty (Lightfoot et al., 2013; Rose, 2010; Tyack & Cuban, 1997). Specifically for Black and Native American or Indigenous students, educational access remained out of reach until decades later. President Lyndon B. Johnson's War on Poverty and landmark 1965 Head Start project centered intensive family supports (e.g., parenting education, home visiting, nutritious foods, early intervention for disabilities, etc.) that strengthened early math and literacy performance, career trajectory, and family functioning (Chaudry et al., 2017; HHS, 2018) with broad influence on children's academic skills, child mortality, and outcomes at later stages of the life span (Currie & Thomas, 1995; Puma et al., 2010). This federal initiative also provided mental health and targeted counseling for participating children and their families facing financial vulnerability.

The authors will review four seminal cases in education that have impacted racial/ethnic minoritized children:

- *Brown v. Board of Education* Supreme Court Case (1954);
- *Plessy v. Ferguson* Supreme Court Case;
- Carl D. Perkins Education Act or Perkins Act (1984); and
- *Plyer v. Doe* (1972).

Brown v. Board of Education *(1954)*

In America, education rights have been won through legal wins including *Brown v. Board of Education* (1954) initiated in Topeka, Kansas. This 1954 decision addressed persistent gaps in teaching and education resources sighted in a series of momentum-building cases for Mexican-American, African American, and Asian-American children in segregated schools decades earlier (Crandall & Bailey, 2018; Ovando & Combs, 2018). While the Brown decision led to more *focus* on racial differences in schools, the inadequacy of school resources has not lessened for some student groups (Baker et al., 2016; Barton & Coley, 2010; Chaudry et al., 2017). Today, school systems may contend with re-segregation, discrimination, and unwelcoming environments even for our youngest children (García Coll et al., 1996; Neblett et al., 2009). Issues of poor school quality and institutional threats such as inappropriate placement into special education services, exclusionary discipline, and tracking out of enrichment still weaken gains in meaningful school integration, student well-being, and academic performance for historically racial/ethnic minoritized children.

Notably, the *Brown v. Board* decision led to gains in targeted early childhood and special education access for young children and their families experiencing poverty. Federal poverty-based programs like Early Head Start and Head Start, along with the increasing number of state and district kindergarten and pre-kindergarten initiatives, have promoted school readiness in early math, literacy, communication, prosocial behavior, and physical development. Post-*Brown*, these early childhood programs became linked to *Title I* services and empowered many schools to prioritize parenting goals, multilingualism, and disability intervention (CCSSO, 2017).

Many school districts have experienced waves of demographic shifts and backlash against school integration in large and suburban, mid-size districts where communities reluctantly integrated over the years (Williams & Graham, 2020). For example, the *Brown v. Board of Education* decision (1954) led to a firestorm of "Massive Resistance" and haphazard integration by Virginia school systems. Compelled by persistent parent and civil rights advocacy, Alexandria City Public Schools Superintendent John Albohlm acquiesced to school desegregation at T.C. Williams High School in 1971. This district, like others, has continued to evolve and grapple with serving children and families from various racial-ethnic backgrounds since that time (Reed, 2014).

Plessy v. Ferguson *(1896)*

This case affirmed "separate but equal" as the basis for the piecemeal expansion of school desegregation before the *Brown v. Board of Education* (1954) decision. Still, history shows that disparate textbook resources and school access were prevalent for African American, Mexican-American, Asian, Native, and Indigenous children before and after *Plessy v. Ferguson* (Rose, 2010; Tyack & Cuban, 1997). Givens (2021) emphasizes the detriment of persistent anti-literacy laws and Black codes which outlawed the education of Black people in the face of resistance:

> Anti-Literacy laws and the intellectual surveillance that accompanied them left great marks on the politics of Black education ... While the overwhelming majority of Blacks were illiterate under slavery, approximately 10% learned to read and/or write, suggesting that literate slaves were not unusual. These literate slaves were recognized as leaders with a practical skillset that benefited their community. (p. 27–28)

Essentially, this functional and communal role as teachers represents the earliest mechanism through which the education of Black children took place within family and fictive kin networks of free and enslaved persons. These judicial and legislative shifts greatly impacted collective actions to desegregate public schools into most of the 20th century. Home-based, neighborhood, and informal care options were the norm, particularly for Black families who faced employment demands and economic disadvantage if children attended school at all.

Carl D. Perkins Education Act or Perkins Act *(1984)*

The school counseling field shifted to focus on professional competencies and student outcomes related to college entrance, career readiness, and the assessment of student career needs more broadly with the enactment of the Carl D. Perkins Education Act orPerkins Act of 1984 (Friedel, 2006). This landmark legislation legitimized the term *school counseling program* (Herr, 2001, p. 241) and added new dimensions to the purview of school counseling programs by mandating that schools accomplish the following objectives:

1   Acquire self-assessment, career planning, decision-making, and employability skills;
2   Make the transition of education and training to work;
3   Maintain marketability of job skills in established occupations;
4   Develop new skills to move away from declining occupational fields and enter new and emerging fields in high-technology areas and fields experiencing skill shortages;
5   Develop mid-career job search skills and clarify career goals; and
6   Obtain and use information on financial assistance for postsecondary and vocational education and job training (Title III, Section 521, [4]).

In coordination with the recent Every Student Succeeds Act (2015) reauthorization of federal education policy, the Perkins Act defines many of the responsibilities and priorities of school counselors.

Plyler v. Doe *Supreme Court Case (1972)*

A lawsuit was filed against the Texas Education Code (457 U.S. 202) in violation of the Fourteenth Amendment and Equal Protection Clause of the U.S. Constitution. The State of Texas revised the education law in 1975 to withhold district state funds from local schools for children of undocumented immigrants, allowing the schools to deny enrollment to children who did not enter the U.S. legally (Baczynski, 2013; Harmon et al., 2010). The law was overturned by the U.S. Supreme Court in 1982, prohibiting states from denying a free K–12 education to undocumented students (Diaz-Strong et al., 2011; Gonzales et al., 2015; Harmon et al., 2010). School districts and personnel are no longer allowed to deny immigrant children access to education, nor may they request documentation of immigrant status. Denying undocumented students access to education takes an "inestimable toll on the social, economic, intellectual and psychological well-being of the individual" (Plyler v. Doe, 1982, para. 3). *Plyler v. Doe* addressed access to K–12 education, while immigration reform and access to post-secondary education remained a concern.

Historical Impact of Institutional/Systemic Racism

Social injustice within our country (e.g., inequities in housing, education, health, governmental policies, policing, and so forth) directly affects students and families from all backgrounds in schools. These injustices clearly impact some minoritized families based on their socio-historical experiences, biological vulnerabilities, and intergenerational trauma interwoven with long-standing racial and socio-economic disparities present in hyper-segregated and racially excluded school communities (Bankston & Caldas, 1996; Holcomb-McCoy, 2021; Shonkoff et al., 2021; Trent et al., 2019). Bankston and Caldas, nearly 30 years ago, found that the degree to which Black students attended racially segregated schools after *Brown v. Board of Education* had a compelling negative influence on academic achievement outcomes (e.g., assessment results). At the time, this was not necessarily influenced by socioeconomic factors, as both Black and white students were negatively affected by this racial segregation in school settings (Figure 3.2).

As counselors, we want to acknowledge and be aware of the impact segregation and the integration of schools have on the students and families we serve. Research offers that racial/ethnic minorities, specifically Black families, have understandable hesitation about the school system. Historical literature is often taught incorrectly or omitted. Implicit biases that have remained throughout generations have resulted in unfair discipline policies and the overrepresentation of Black children in Special Education.

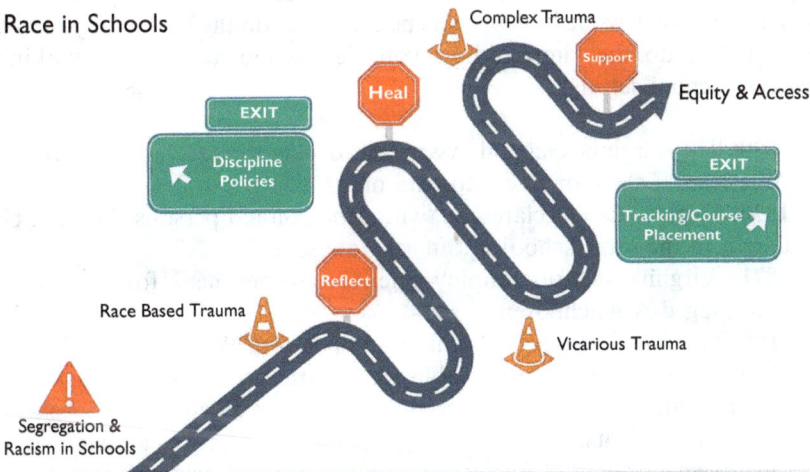

Race in Schools

Figure 3.2 Manifestations of institutional/systemic racism in and out of schools.

Furthermore, schools often engage in a tracking system that restricts high-achieving Black children from enrolling in gifted coursework. To combat these inequities school counselors are encouraged to:

Continuously reflect on their own biases, acknowledging that this process is lifelong;

Continue to gain knowledge of the impact racism and systemic oppression have on school systems;

Examine current policies and procedures for bias;

Develop a data-driven school counseling program that fosters inclusivity and calls out instances of bias in student success;

Address and challenge the status quo, identifying innovative ways to ensure their school counseling program is equitable, encouraging, and centers the needs of diverse populations;

Challenge faculty and staff to review their own bias and the impact it has on their work with students;

Establish accountability measures for all faculty, staff, and students to uphold the school's commitment to inclusive excellence; and

Reimagine a school environment that is trauma-informed, inclusive, and accessible to meet the needs of diverse learners.

Consider the timeline of events below. For 128 years, Black people have historically encountered racist policies with long-standing effects, especially in the state of Virginia, where the authors reside. All three authors attended schools across the developmental spectrum (elementary, middle, high school, undergraduate, graduate school, and Ph.D.) in Virginia. With this in mind, review the bullet points below. What do they mean to you? To what extent do they impact how you view school counselors working within a school setting?

- **1830**: The Virginia General Assembly forbids the teaching of African Americans – slave or free – to read or write.
- **1870**: Virginia Law declares ... "white and colored persons shall not be taught in the same school but in separate schools ... ."
- **1871**: Virginia schools employ one "Negro teacher" for every 232 school-aged A.A. children.
- **1890**: The first "colored" schoolhouses opened in Winter Park, Florida.
- **1896**: *Plessy vs. Ferguson* established separate schools for Black and White children. Black schools were under-financed, with fewer teachers, too many students, and inadequate resources. There was an average of one "Negro teacher" for every 80 school-aged A.A. children.
- **1954**: *Brown v. Board of Education* rules racial segregation in schools unconstitutional.

- **1956**: The "Southern Manifesto" was signed by more than one hundred congressmen opposing integrated schools (including Virginia). The Massive resistance to prevent integration began on February 25 of that year.
- **1958**: Schools in Warren County, Charlottesville, and Norfolk were seized and closed to prevent integration. The VA Supreme Court later overturned the school-closing law.
- **1964**: Only 5% of Black students in Virginia were attending integrated schools.

Discussion Activity

Think about the students attending the schools that you are familiar with, using the following questions as prompts:

1 If the state in which you lived decided to refrain from funding students from different underrepresented racial and minoritized backgrounds or citizenship status, what do you hypothesize these students would look like?
2 What could a school counselor do within their purview to support these students? What areas of advocacy would need to be targeted to address this disgraceful issue?
3 How willing are you to engage in a fight for equity and justice in schools, even if you may be choosing a less politically popular stance on an issue?
4 Schools will continue to see increases in the number of undocumented students and immigrant/mixed-status families they serve. How will you prepare for this reality?

In addition to reflecting on the activity above, we must understand the ways in which social stratification shapes interactions with students today. We situate the role of a school counselor within the broader body of knowledge on education history, school counseling program delivery in schools, and education policy related to students from racially and ethnically vulnerable backgrounds (see Figure 3.1). An interdisciplinary approach grounds our understanding of previous school counseling interventions for these key populations. Reflect on the role school counselors play in addressing disparities experienced by racial/ethnic minorities in schools with an intersectional lens.

Reflection

1 To what extent do the questions above remain unanswered?
2 What roles do race and gender play in the outcomes of these inquiries?

3 What can school counselors do today that intersects with these historical questions?

4 Read Diane's story below and then revisit questions 2 and 3 above. How are your responses now?

Diane's Story: Integration and the Sinister Truth

It is not who you attend school with, but who controls the school you attend. – Nikki Giovanni

The quote above speaks to my sentiments about my past experiences and informs my current thoughts about the impact integration has had on education. It has been more than six decades since the landmark Supreme Court decision in *Brown v. Board of Education of Topeka*. Why is this significant to me? Well, I was a key player in the desegregation of schools in the state of Georgia – well, at least in my school district, known as Candler County Public Schools. When this landmark decision was handed down from the Supreme Court, Georgia, like several southern states, adopted a position of massive resistance to desegregation. As a matter of fact, Governor Ernest Vandiver made segregation the focal point of his 1958 campaign, promising to maintain the institution of being separate. State law-makers issued an ultimatum to Black people to leave the NAACP or lose their teaching licenses. The question for me now is: *how much has this attitude across the public education landscape changed?*

At the time of the Brown v. Board of Education decision, 109 of Georgia's public school districts had been involved in litigation over school desegregation. Candler County Public Schools was one of those school districts. Candler County remains under court-order status with the U.S. District Court.

Candler County School District

Candler County is located in the east-central part of the state. The county comprises one school district, and there are five schools in the district. The district is mixed racially and has a total enrollment of about 1,900 students. White people make up the largest racial group, comprising just over half of total enrollment, while Black people comprise about one-third of all students, and Latinos about 15%. The district has been under court jurisdiction since 1969, and, according to a representative for the district, the district will not be seeking unitary status.[1]

Initiating Case Name: U.S. v. State of Georgia, et al., C.A. No. 12972
Year of Initiating Case: 1969
Issue: School Desegregation
Current Status: Under Court Order

I was a middle school student selected to begin the integration process of Candler County Public Schools. I was part of a group of students who were identified as performing in the top 10% of their class. At the time, I could not decide if it was a blessing or a curse to be a part of this group. I felt a sense of safety and pride being in the company of people who looked like me and nurtured my potential to be an outstanding student.

Integration did not make me feel good about "being included," because I knew that there was no sincerity in the endeavor. Integration was being forced on a group of state lawmakers, local school administrators, and parents who were openly defying the legal ruling of the U.S. Supreme Court! I was not sure I would be respected or recognized as a student of great academic acumen. I was not sure I would be challenged academically. I was not sure I would be afforded the same educational experiences that White students had been given and would continue to have. I was not sure I would be disciplined fairly. I was not sure that I would be safe. Unfortunately, there were acts of racism that gave birth to these thoughts of uncertainty, thereby elevating my fears about integration and its intent to create equity within the educational system.

As part of the initial group to "go to the White school," I found myself abandoned on the playground a lot. I did not understand why the White students would come and collect my friends, who came with me to the White school, to play with them but leave me behind. There was one White female who did the opposite. She befriended me, and we spent many recesses together on the playground. One day, she called me to tell me that two girls from the White contingency had told her that she should not play with me because she might turn Black. You see, my skin tone was darker than that of my friends who had come to the White school with me. Another distinguishing factor was that their moms were either teachers or nurses, while my mother was the wife of a farmer and had only an elementary education. As a matter of fact, both of my parents had to leave school to work on their respective farms to help sustain their families. Even in this effort to integrate, I was being segregated.

Once the school system had been fully integrated, I witnessed Black students get paddled in a way that reminded me of the movies and stories that my parents had shared with me about slavery. This was especially true of Black boys. They were always disciplined more harshly than White boys who had committed similar acts in breaking school rules. I remember vividly the time that I was paddled by a Black teacher because I hit a White male student who had stomped my foot with his cleated football shoes. He was not disciplined for what he had done to me. At the time, I was hurt and angry because of the unfairness of the situation. In my adult years when I reflected on the incident, I concluded that however wrong she was, she was just afraid of the "system" as I was. I decided that if she had paddled that White male student, her career as a teacher would have ended that day. So, she made the decision that I could be sacrificed, so that she could continue to be a teacher. I guess this is what is called "taking one for the team."

While I know that integration matters and has resulted in significant change, I still find myself questioning whether its intent has been fully realized even now. Has integration truly achieved the level of equality and equity in education that resulted from the *Brown* decision? From my experiences of being a parent of school-age children, from experiences as a professional who worked with schools, from my experiences as a school counselor practicing in schools, and now as a counselor educator preparing students to enter the profession, I cannot honestly answer this question with a definitive yes.

In our current political climate, some of the barriers that *Brown* enacted to tear down appear to be very much present today. There are still challenges with certain racial and ethnic groups having access to the curriculum and support that will ensure their academic success. The inequities and disparities in other systems have a direct, and, sometimes indirect, impact on the equal and equitable opportunity of access in the school setting. In many school districts, you may find that enrollment of Black students is more disproportionately represented in Special Education than in AP and honors courses. You will also find that zip codes determine the amount and ways in which financial support and resources are allocated in a school district. You will find that Black students, especially Black males, are more likely to be suspended or expelled from school than White males. You will also find that Black girls are "pushed out," "dress-coded," and adultified more often than White females. Is there anything new under the sun?

Pedro Noguera (2019) stated in his article "Why Integration Matters":

It is time to regenerate our commitment to the promise of the *Brown* decision and remind all who doubt its importance why it still matters. There is no doubt that what happens in our nation's schools will play a major role in determining the type of nation we become. Given the current state of affairs in our nation and our schools, we have good reason to be concerned. Let's not take this issue lightly.

(Noguera, 2019, section 5; para. 3)

In summary, Dr. Noguera's perspective resonates with me. While I may have some skepticism about integration and its impact on changing the educational landscape, I cannot deny that it matters. This is a diverse society where we cannot escape the need for our children to be prepared to live and work successfully together. *Because it matters, it is imperative that we collectively understand that it truly does not matter who children attend school with, but who controls the school they attend.* History should not find us doing the same thing, making the same mistakes and excuses. We know better; we need to do better.

Summary

This chapter contains a brief overview of American history related to vulnerable groups of students and education policies that have impacted school counseling in America. This was no easy task. Though not an exhaustive history, we selected landmark events and benchmarks that shape student experiences in schools today. The field ultimately seeks to promote comprehensive mental health services, authentic and meaningful assessment of student's academic, socio-emotional, and career growth, and comprehensive school counseling programs to realize these goals. The work continues! With this important knowledge in mind, we consider the school counseling profession a platform to align your values and actions to create healthy and safe schools. Acknowledging the truth of our nation's dark, deeply embedded history with racism may fuel a desire and bolster school counselor advocacy. The timeliness of this work evidences the surging interest in social-justice-oriented school counseling and the need to further examine its benefits and the risks to its pursuit.

Key Takeaways

1 It is important to understand the impact that court laws at the local and national levels can have on U.S. school systems.
2 Developing inclusive practices within school counseling is essential, and there are many ways to accomplish this outcome.
3 Identifying ways to address and combat disparities experienced by racial/ethnic minoritized students in K–12 schools is essential for school counselors.

Chapter Application

1 What did school counseling look like historically and who were the students and families being served?

2 Identify disparities in your school. Are they connected to the racial/ ethnic makeup of your students?

3 What is the history of the county you work in? When was it integrated? How does the past impact your school system presently?

4 Using the figure within this chapter, examine the gap in movements between 1970 and 2013. Explore legislative racism (i.e., Zero tolerance, mandatory minimums, War on Drugs, School-to-Prison Pipeline). What impact does this have on Black students today? How have past and present movements impacted, or been impacted by, this particular period of time?

Note

1 *Desegregation of Public School Districts in Georgia: 35 Public Schools Districts Have Unitary Status; 74 Districts Remain Under Court* Jurisdiction, Georgia Advisory Committee to the United States Commission on Civil Rights, December 2007; Melissa Williams, Director of Technology, Vocation, and Personnel, Candler County School District, letter to Peter Minarik, March 6, 2006, Southern Regional Office, USCCR, files.

Reference

Baczynski, D. (2013). Education connection: The chilling effects of student immigration tracking systems violate Plyler. *Children's Legal Rights Journal, 33*, 212.

Baker, B.D., Farrie, D., & Sciarra, D.G. (2016). Mind the Gap: 20 Years of progress and retrenchment in school funding and achievement gaps. *ETS Research Report Series, 16*(1), 1–37. 10.1002/ets2.12098

Barton, P.E. & Coley, R.J. (2010). The Black-White achievement gap: When progress stopped. Princeton, NJ: Educational Testing Services. ETS Policy Information Center Report. https://origin-www.ets.org/research/policy_ research_reports/publications/report/2010/igxu

Brown v. Board of Education. (1954). 347 U.S. 483 (1954).

Bankston III, C., & Caldas, S. J. (1996). Majority African American schools and social injustice: The influence of de facto segregation on academic achievement. *Social Forces, 75*(2), 535–555.

Carl, D. Perkins Vocational Act of 1984 (PL 98–524). *United States statutes at large*. Washington, DC: Government Printing Office.

Chaudry, A., Morrissey, T., Weiland, C., & Yoshikawa, H. (2017). *Cradle to Kindergarten: A New plan to combat inequality*. New York: Russell Sage Foundation. ISBN: 9780871545572

Council of Chief State School Officers. (2017). *New early childhood coordination requirements in the Every Student Succeeds Act (ESSA)*: A Toolkit for state and local educational agencies, head start programs, and the early childhood field. Washington, DC: https://ccsso.org/resource-library/new-early-childhood-coordination-requirements-every-student-succeeds-act-essa

Crandall, J. & Bailey, K. M. (Eds.). (2018). *Global perspectives on language education policies*. Abingdon: Routledge.

Currie, J., & Thomas, D. (1995). Does Head Start make a difference? *American Economic Review, 85*, 341–364.

Diaz-Strong, D., Gómez, C., Luna-Duarte, M. E., & Meiners, E. R. (2011). Purged: Undocumented students, financial aid policies, and access to higher education. *Journal of Hispanic Higher Education, 10*(2), 107–119.

Evans-Winters, V., Hines, D.E., Moore, A., & Jones, T.L. (2018). Locating Black girls in educational policy discourse: Implications for the every student succeeds act. *Teachers College Record, 120*(13), 1–18.

Every Student Succeeds Act, 20 U.S.C. § 6301 (2015).

Friedel, J.N. (2006). Where has vocational education gone? The impact of federal legislation on the expectations, design, and function of vocational education as reflected in the reauthorization of the Carl D. Perkins Career and Technical Education Act of 2006. *American Educational History Journal, 38*(1), 37–53.

García Coll, C., Lamberty, G., Jenkins, R., McAdoo, H. Crnic, K., Wasik, B., & Garcia, H. (1996). An integrative model for the study of developmental competencies in minority children. *Child Development, 67*, 1891–1914. doi:10.1111/j.1467-8624.1996.tb01834.x

Georgia Advisory Committee to the United States Commission on Civil Rights. (2007, December). *Desegregation of public school districts in Georgia: 35 public school districts have unitary status, 74 districts remain under court jurisdiction.* https://www.usccr.gov/files/pubs/docs/GADESG-FULL.pdf

Gilliam, W. S., Maupin, A. N., Reyes, C. R., Accavitti, M., & Shic, F. (2016). *Do early educators' implicit biases regarding sex and race relate to behavior expectations and recommendations of preschool expulsions and suspensions.* New Haven: Yale Child Study Center.

Givens, J. R. (2021). *Fugitive Pedagogy: Carter G. Woodson and the art of Black teaching*. Cambridge, MA: Harvard University Press.

Gonzales, R. G., Heredia, L. L., & Negrón-Gonzales, G. (2015). Untangling Plyler's legacy: Undocumented students, schools, and citizenship. *Harvard Educational Review, 85*(3), 318–341.

González, N. (2004). Disciplining the discipline: Anthropology and the pursuit of quality education. *Educational Researcher, 33*(5), 17–25. doi:10.3102/00131 89X033005017

Greenberg, E. & Monarrez, T. (2019). *Segregated from the start: Comparing segregation in early childhood and K–12 education*. Washington: The Urban Institute. Retrieved from https://www.urban.org/features/segregated-start

Griffith, A., Hurd, N., & Hussain, S. (2017). "I Didn't Come to School for This": A Qualitative examination of experiences with race-related stressors and coping responses among Black students attending a predominantly White institution. *Journal of Adolescent Research, 34*(2), 115–139. doi:10.1177/0743558417742983

Gysbers, N. C. (2001). School guidance and counseling in the 21st century: Remember the past into the future. *Professional School Counseling, 5*(2), 96–105.

Harmon, C., Carne, G., Lizardy-Hajbi, K., & Wilkerson, E. (2010). Access to higher education for undocumented students: "Outlaws" of social justice, equity, and equality. *Journal of Praxis in Multicultural Education, 5*(1), 9. doi:10.9741/2161-2978.1033

Herr, E. L. (2001). The Impact of national policies, economics, and school reform on comprehensive guidance programs. *Professional School Counseling, 4*(4), 236–245.

Holcomb-McCoy, C. (Ed.). (2021). *Antiracist counseling in schools and communities.* Alexandria, VA: American Counseling Association Publications.

Iruka, I. U., Durden, T. R., Gardner-Neblett, N., Ibekwe-Okafor, N., Sansbury, A., & Telfer, N. A. (2021). Attending to the adversity of racism against young Black children. *Policy Insights from the Behavioral and Brain Sciences*, 1–8. doi:10.1177/23727322211029313

Lightfoot, C., Cole, M., & Cole. S. (2013). *The development of children* (7th ed.). New York: Worth.

Neblett, E.W., Chavous, T.M., Nguyen, H. X., Sellers, R.M. (2009). "Say It Loud-I'm Black and I'm Proud": Parents' messages about race, racial discrimination, and academic achievement in African American boys. *Journal of Negro Education, 78*(3), 246–259, 362-363.

Noguera, P. (2019, April 1). *Why school integration matters.* The Association for Supervision and Curriculum Development. https://www.ascd.org/el/articles/why-school-integration-matters

Ovando, C. J. & Combs, M.C. (2018). Policy and Programs. In C. Ovando & M.C. Combs (Eds.), *Bilingual and ESL classrooms* (6th ed.) (pp. 39–78). Lanham: Rowman & Littlefield.

Plyler v. Doe, 457 U.S. 202, 1982.

Puma, M., Bell, S., Cook, R., Heid, C., Shapiro, G., Broene, P., Jenkins, F., Fletcher, P., Quinn, L., Friedman, J., Ciarico, J., Rohacek, M., Adams, G., Spier, E. (2010). *The Head Start impact study final report.* Washington: Office of Planning, Research and Evaluation Administration for Children and Families U.S. Department of Health and Human Services.

Reed, D. S. (2014). *Building the federal schoolhouse: Localism and the American education state.* New York: Oxford University Press.

Rose, E. (2010). *The promise of preschool: From Head Start to universal pre-kindergarten.* New York: Oxford University Press. ISBN: 9780199926459

Shonkoff, J. P., Slopen, N., & Williams, D.L. (2021). Early childhood adversity, toxic stress, and the impacts of racism on the foundations of health. *Annual Review of Public Health, 42*, 115–134. doi:10.1146/annurev-publhealth-090419-101940

Trent, M., Dooley, D., Dougé, J., Section on Adolescent Health, Council on Community Pediatrics, & Committee on Adolescence (2019). The Impact of racism on child and adolescent health. *Pediatrics, 144*(2), 1–14. doi:10.1542/peds.2019-1765

Tyack, D.B. & Cuban, L. (1997). *Tinkering toward Utopia: A century of public school reform.* Cambridge, MA: Harvard University Press.

U.S. Department of Health and Human Services (HHS), Administration for Children and Families, Office of Head Start, National Center on Parent, Family, and Community Engagement. (2018). *Head start parent, family, and community engagement framework*. Washington, D.C.: The United States Department of Health and Human Services. Retrieved online from https://eclkc.ohs.acf.hhs.gov/school-readiness/article/head-start-parent-family-community-engagement-framework

Williams, S.M., & Graham, J. (2020). Cross-racial interactions in schools 65 years after *Brown*. *Peabody Journal of Education*, *94*(5), 545–554. 10.1080/0161956X.2019.1668211

Chapter 4

Preparing the School Counselor for Advocacy

Developing a Theoretical Framework for Action

Key Terms (See Chapter 1)
Critical Consciousness, Social Justice

Author Narrative: Sam Steen

As students, we are exposed to some of our society's most oppressive institutions, namely public schools in this country. I was the first to go to college in my family, and the construction of my identity and my viewpoints about education were directly influenced by the messages I received from my parents. I now see my experiences within the Triple Quandary theory and Schooling of African Americans (Boykin, 1986) which embodies how I was raised by my parents. This assumption relates to how I was socialized as an African American in this country. This theory entails a process of racial socialization and the patterns associated with understanding: a) the American Dream; b) Black culture (specifically referring to knowledge of one's African heritage); and c) what it means to be Black in an oppressive society. I would say that in part, I received all of these messages, yet not through a lens of Black empowerment or based on the latest research for African Americans. I was taught these ideals because "that was just the way things were," according to my parents. I recall my parents instilling in me that the "American Dream" was achievable by anyone and that education was the key. One specific message given by my mother was "the harder you work now in school, the less work you'll have to do in the future." Alternatively, "if you don't work hard now in school, then the work you'll do in the future will be even more difficult." Moreover, the latter two components of this theory were also reflected primarily by my mother's wisdom. She would regularly tell me that regardless of my circumstances or abilities, I was still a Black man, and therefore needed to work harder than my non-Black peers. Again, I do not recall any clear explanation as to why I needed to understand this. There were some exceptions to my racial status: she would explain that it was necessary to be diligent in my studies and to

DOI: 10.4324/9781003226253-5

stay out of trouble because we were Christians. This Christianity also meant that working hard, being productive, and getting along with all people were honorable actions. We never discussed the discriminatory aspects of Christianity nor the complexities associated with the Bible being used to justify slavery.

Today, I have conflicting messages that I work through regularly during my own spiritual journey. One poignant message that I realize now, which also was not explicitly stated or explained was the pressure to conform to masculinity – to act like a man, even at a young age. This message on manhood was stated by my father in particular. In addition to statements like "men are tough," I observed from my father that men don't cry, especially Black men. I recall seeing him cry only once! And this exception was when I was a third-grader. This pursuit of strength and Black manhood over the years resulted in attempts to hide my vulnerabilities, never publicly sharing my tears, avoiding asking for help, and never letting anyone know my fears. These direct and indirect messages from my father did provide a foundation of resiliency, but this shell masked the underlying terror and fear of failure and my ability to be authentic. Now, I wonder how my aforementioned familial, gender, cultural, and racial socialization messages – including preparing to face racial barriers, stereotypes, and biases, narrowly focused spiritual exploration, egalitarianism in terms of diligence and working hard for success, and so forth – impact both my past and current views, work ethic, and professional dispositions. Undoubtedly my past school experiences inform my work as a school counselor advocate, but it is less clear how influential my upbringing is. This area requires further self-exploration.

Content

We aim to re-imagine school counseling frameworks that are needed to interrogate how we view and support all students. We must fundamentally challenge the racist underpinnings and nature of schooling in the U.S. as discussed in the previous chapters. We must intervene, advocate, and implement responsive strategies with a conscientious outlook.

Social Justice in Schools: A Brief Historical Review

The historical context of barriers to education for diverse populations allows us to examine the insidious nature of discriminatory practices in the educational system. Systemic inequities in schools such as inaccessible education, segregation, and boarding schools that fostered the erasure of culture, have a present-day impact. At times the often-used term social justice can be unclear and even fuel anger, fear, or hatred. We present some documentation of the history of social justice within education in the United States.

Nearly a century ago, there was a call for teachers to build a new social order (Counts, 1932). Counts invited educators to think more expansively when it came to U.S. public education, society at large, and the influence of educators in shaping a more democratic and just country, and encouraged educators to see themselves as political actors who can shape their environments (e.g., family, school, and community) through their work (Lugg & Shoho, 2006). Others have challenged the status quo by demonstrating that educational spaces can illuminate the ills of capitalism, examine true democracy, and create liberated thinkers who are not afraid of change and who see the world as fluid and based on realities (Friere, 1968; 2000). More specifically, Freire pointed to the political nature of schooling and the intersection of teacher, student, and society. Next, critical pedagogies (e.g., CRT, feminism, queer theory, etc.) in the spirit of social justice seek to empower minoritized students who continue to be subjected to oppressive school environments, policies, and practices. These critical pedagogies challenge inequities while offering insight, strategies, and opportunities for creative discourse that dismantles long-standing and narrowly focused education primarily favoring White students.

Nearly 30 years ago, scholars provided great clarity on the necessity of seeing equity and social justice in school as both the journey and the destination (e.g., process and goal, Bell, 1994, p. 3). Bell notes that participation is required for all groups and is co-created to ensure that all benefit from participating within a society that fulfills everyone's needs (Bell, 1994). Two decades ago, authors called for students to take an active role in their education and for teachers to create empowering yet critical educational environments (Hackman, 2005). In other words, taking on this type of disposition of addressing systemic oppression requires examining and challenging practices and policies (Murrell, 2006). Social justice within schools requires using a lens through which social, political, and economic problems are examined while collectively combating these systems to be more equitable and inclusive.

Racial Demographics and Racial Exploration

In schools across the country, a staggering disconnect exists between the racial makeup of the student population and the school counselors serving them. Currently, 66% of school counselors report that they are White and female, with racial/ethnic minoritized school counselors reporting a collective 24% (American School Counselor Association, 2021). In contrast, researchers and research institutes continue to confirm that within the U.S. the majority of Pre-K-12 students hold racially and ethnically minoritized status (McFarland et al., 2018).

In the study referenced above, sponsored by ASCA, the researchers sought the experiences of ASCA members to gain a general understanding of the practices of school counselors and schools in supporting diversity, equity, and inclusion (DEI), and in addressing racism and bias. What they found was that many schools lack DEI curricula/programs and reported limited success at addressing disproportionalities and improving students' understanding of racism and bias. We would argue that the students will follow the lead of the school counselors. In other words, in order to teach children and adolescents, whose racial and ethnic backgrounds span a wide spectrum about racism and bias:

1 School counselors will need to do their own internal exploration and honest reflection to understand these concepts in real and personal ways and to use this insight to help others, no matter their racial heritage; and
2 School counselors' focus should not be solely on teaching students about racism and bias, but must offer students a platform to share with school counselors, faculty, and staff, their personal experiences with racism and bias.

We are certain from our personal and professional experiences that engaging students and family members in DEI work that focuses on race is quite difficult, especially now. This study and others affirm this reality. For instance, Ieva and colleagues report findings on school counselors' use of group counseling interventions to combat racism in schools. In this study, half of the participating school counselors reported that they did address racism directly, and the other half reported that they did not – neither did they create group interventions that took into account power, privilege, and intersectionality (Ieva et al., 2022). The researchers within the afore-mentioned ASCA study concluded that the majority of the school coun-selor survey respondents expressed concerns regarding resistance from parents and local communities, preventing successful engagement and delivery of interventions and programs that could lead to uprooting dis-proportionalities. We should not blame students, families, and communi-ties for a lack of success in this meaningful and controversial work. Rather, school counselors can seek to work collaboratively, creatively, and effec-tively to foster culturally responsive and sustainable programs.

School counselors' steep learning curve in working with students from racially or ethnically minoritized backgrounds has been a pervasive problem throughout the profession's evolution. Moreover, the recruitment and retention of racial/ethnically diverse school counselors further widen the gap in how we can best serve students of similar backgrounds. It is important to note that we desire to celebrate race and culture in a way that captures the potential beauty we all can offer. We aim to make no as-sumptions that racially minoritized school counselors can only work with Black and Brown students and that White school counselors cannot suc-cessfully work with students who have different races and cultures.

Cultural Emphases

It is commonly accepted that culture often refers to ethnic identity (e.g., shared history, language, religion, or national origin) that can encompass single or various racial groups. We assert that school counselors have an ethical obligation to serve their student population fairly and equitably. They must ensure that students have access to quality education that is inclusive, recognizing the strengths reflected in diversity. The American Counseling Association (ACA's) Multicultural and Social Justice Counseling Competencies (MSJCC), summarized below, offers a framework for school and clinical mental health counselors to engage in culturally competent work.

Multicultural and Social Justice Counseling Competencies

The MSJCC (Figure 4.1) is a conceptual framework that provides counselors with competencies in the areas of multiculturalism and social justice. The framework is composed of four quadrants that "highlight the intersection of identities and the dynamics of power, privilege, and oppression

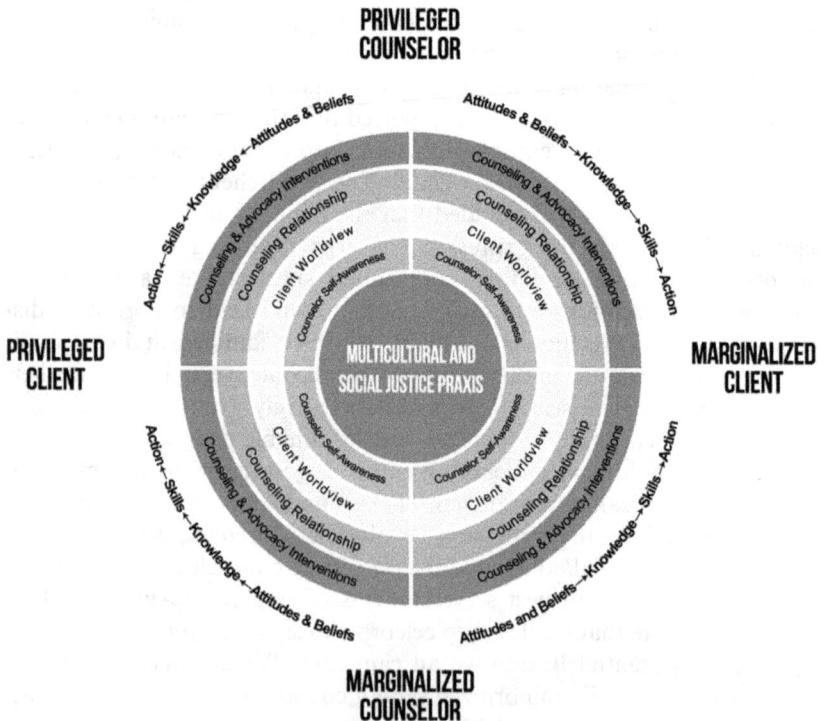

Figure 4.1 Multicultural and Social Justice Counseling Competencies.

that influence the counseling relationship" (p. 3). Within the framework are four developmental domains: (1) counselor self-awareness; (2) client worldview; (3) counseling relationship; and (4) counseling and advocacy interventions. Within the first three domains are the following competencies: attitudes and beliefs, knowledge, skills, and action (AKSA). School counselors who hold a privileged or minoritized identity should develop a self-awareness that explores their social identity, concepts of power, privilege, oppression, strengths, and limitations.

Multiculturally competent school counselors acknowledge the assumptions, beliefs, values, and worldviews they hold as privileged or minoritized individuals by acknowledging their identity, status in society, and the influence of their worldview. Through increased self-awareness, school counselors are better equipped to serve students of a diverse population. In addition to self-awareness, counselors are encouraged to develop an understanding of how historical systems of privilege and oppression have shaped the way individuals are treated in society. Further exploration of knowledge allows school counselors to gain a better understanding of the advantages and disadvantages of their students. By increasing their self-awareness and knowledge, counselors broaden their skills. The MSJCC posits that counselors should acquire critical thinking, communication, application, analytical, and evaluation skills in their work with clients/students.

The final competency (Ratts et al., 2016) is *action;* counselors should take action through courageous conversation, using broaching strategies (Jones & Galdy, 2022) to explore student/counselor identities and their impact on the counseling relationship (DayVines et al., 2022). Specifically, DayVines and colleagues discovered that school counselor trainees who were less comfortable with their own racial identity (i.e., held lower levels of racial identity functioning) were less likely to successfully broach attitudes and behaviors than those with higher levels of racial identity. We discuss more on the Broaching model in a subsequent chapter.

Social Justice Competencies

In addition to the MSJCC, Constantine et al. (2007) developed nine social justice competencies. The social justice competencies encourage counselors to: 1) increase knowledge of how social injustices are experienced at individual, cultural, and societal levels; 2) actively self-reflect on issues of race, ethnicity, oppression, power, and privilege; 3) remain self-aware of how their power and privilege parallel experiences with oppression and injustice; 4) challenge interventions that hinder and exploit the well-being of individuals and groups; 5) increase knowledge of Indigenous models of health and healing; 6) increase awareness of global issues and injustices; 7) develop and implement preventive interventions therapeutically; 8) collaborate with community stakeholders for culturally relevant services; and 9) refine systemic and advocacy skills to promote social change in institutions and communities (Constantine et al., 2007). The social justice competencies complement the MSJCC and further encourage school counselors to be culturally competent and to move towards social justice advocacy.

Decolonizing Therapy

In recent years, the counseling profession has begun exploring the concept of decolonizing therapy. This concept challenges the Eurocentric foundation of the profession and its disregard for diverse populations and the social-political context in which individuals navigate. The profession needs to acknowledge its complicity in the oppression of racial/ethnic minoritized populations. Celebrating *all* populations should be a primary focus in the work of a clinician.

The school counselor, within a decolonized framework, must contend with the inherent bias of a school system and the complicity of school personnel. Their role can either liberate or further oppress the students they serve.

Social Justice Identity Development

Research suggests that the development of a school counselor who advocates a decolonized way of being is an intimate process heavily influenced by the experiences lived by the counselor. Counselor identity development and social justice identity development are intrinsically linked. Professional identity development spans the lifetime of a counselor's career through interpersonal and intrapersonal reflection (Auxier et al., 2003; Brott & Myers, 1999; Gibson et al., 2010). Cyclical in nature, a counselor's identity is ever-evolving (Brott & Myers, 1999). According to Prosek and Hurt (2014), a counselor in training's development is experienced in three stages: 1) identifying a counseling philosophy; 2) applying counseling to practice through an internship or clinical experience; and 3) negotiating or finding congruence with the professional and personal identity. The counselor learns the language and expectations of the profession through observation, consultation, and practice. Though development is constantly evolving, advanced counselors in training will reach a stage of independence and obtain confidence in integrating their professional training with personal attributes (Prosek & Hurt, 2014). Similarly, the experiences of social justice advocates' development evolve through personal and professional experiences. Many school counselors have personal experiences that have motivated them to be just like their own school counselors – or to be better than their school counselors, especially if they had negative experiences attending school as children, adolescents, and young adults.

In addition to personal and professional experiences, there is some research, described below, that is useful in examining how to develop one's social justice identity. The identity of the social justice advocate focuses on consciousness-raising and self-reflection (Singh et al., 2010). Further, traits of the individuals noted within the research include one's personality and ability to understand oppression both intellectually and emotionally (McMahan et al., 2010). Social justice advocates facilitate their own growth by engaging in socially critical thinking, examining how social systems impact others, re-evaluating their own culture and the sociopolitical world (critical consciousness), and moving from oppressive to anti-oppressive thinking through (McAuliffe et al., 2008). Critical consciousness – challenging the socialized worldview of the school counselor themselves – offers a starting point for the development of a social justice identity. We discuss raising one's critical consciousness below, but first, we offer details by Harro (2010a; 2010b), who developed two cyclical frameworks: the Cycle of Socialization and the Cycle of Liberation. These two frameworks bend towards one possible process a school counselor may experience when developing a social justice identity.

Raising Critical Consciousness

Counselors should attend to, be aware of, and be sensitive to biases, discrimination, and oppression (Ratts et al., 2016). Counselors are expected to verbalize and analyze privileges and experiences (Vera & Speight, 2003) and acquire knowledge of how cultural heritage, oppression, racism, and discrimination affect the counselor personally and professionally (Arredondo, 1999). Practitioners who are committed to social justice counseling engage in social critical thinking and critical consciousness, which some have argued unfold along a continuum from oppressive thinking to anti-oppressive thought (Holcomb-McCoy, 2022).

Burgess et al. (2021) investigated the effect of a curriculum that infused critical race pedagogy as a way to raise critical consciousness for adolescents. The authors understood that teaching youth about critical consciousness could precede any tangible action. The study drew from a large pool of youth participants attending school within a northeastern town. The students who identified as Black, Asian, or Hispanic were lumped together as students of color, so their unique experiences were not explored. Nonetheless, the youth who identified as White showed decreases between pre- and post-assessments that measured antiracist attitudes. It is possible that the pre-assessment scores were overinflated, as the young people did not want to be seen as racist so they exaggerated their scores when taking the pre-assessment. However, when taking the post-assessment, perhaps they were being more honest and, therefore, although the scores were lower, they are reflective of true areas for improvement (Burgess et al., 2021).

Socially, critical thinking is the intense analysis of how social structures impact others, particularly minoritized populations. School counselors can understand critical incidents – significant experiences in one's life that prompt them to reevaluate their personal/professional position on socio/political values that could lead to cognitive dissonance. Cognitive dissonance occurs when the experience one has challenges personal and professionally held beliefs (Gorski, 2009). Critical consciousness is the individual's re-evaluation of their own culture and the sociopolitical world – a concept some scholars believe is difficult to achieve. The counselor's movement to anti-oppressive thought begins with self-exploration. A similar suggestion is provided by Harro (2010a; 2010b), who encourages individuals to take inventory of their social identities and relationships for oppression. Research shows that professional identity development is a dynamic, iterative process (Auxier et al., 2003; Brott & Myers, 1999). Conceptual and experiential learning are cyclical processes that assist in the development of a clear professional identity (Auxier et al., 2003).

Cycle of Socialization

Harro (2010a; 2010b) posits that individuals are socialized into various norms from birth that are influenced over time. The concept of socialization includes societal norms that have been taught and further perpetuated over a person's lifetime (Harro, 2010a; 2010b). Cognitive dissonance seeks to disrupt socialization. An individual can move towards liberation or remain wedded to socialized norms.

Cycle of Liberation

The Cycle of Liberation reflects on an individual's interpersonal and intrapersonal processes. Throughout the counselor-in-training's education, reflection is highly encouraged, including personal reflections on social justice and advocacy. Social justice and liberation pedagogies will further solidify the counselor's identity as an advocate. Fostering the social justice identity of counselors leads to multiculturally competent counselors who advocate for others and the profession. Previously discussed research suggests that there are innate traits, coupled with experiences, that propel counselors to advocacy (Caldwell & Vera, 2010; Field & Baker, 2004; McMahan et al., 2010; Singh et al., 2010).

Participants in Caldwell & Vera's (2010), McMahan et al. (2010), and Singh et al. (2010) studies all discussed personal and professional experiences that impacted their work as social justice advocates. Participants also discussed the influence of mentors who served as role models in the counselors' identity development process (Caldwell & Vera, 2010; McMahan et al., 2010). Gibson et al. (2010) propose that to advocate for clients, one must be confident in their professional identity. The social justice identity development of the counselor is an aspect of professional development that has not been thoroughly explored but is expected. The identity of the school counselor is often shaped by the expectations discussed by ASCA in the national model, code of ethics, competencies, and position statements related to diversity and equity. This process of integrating knowledge and emerging skills centers on the theoretical lens through which school counselors understand their role. We continue by exploring these aspects of identity – a primer for the concepts and knowledge that we will introduce to readers in Chapter 5.

With this in mind, the school counseling field must recognize and grapple with a long record of disparities within American education and mental health systems. Three bodies of knowledge inform our understanding and view of this history: a) historical access and navigation of school and mental health systems; b) the role of school counseling in shaping student academic outcomes, college and career readiness, and well-being; and c) the evolving nature of work for school counselors in and out of education settings. Collectively, these areas broaden and deepen school counselors' perspectives on fundamental advocacy issues. Power structures that constrain or facilitate reciprocal, goal-orientated relationships with students – and with their families and communities more broadly – are pathways for alignment. For example, without this framework, school counselors may miss opportunities to incorporate Black students and families' multiple banks of knowledge and liberation (Mayes et al., 2022) or intrinsic, inherited knowledge and skills related to positive racial identity development (Hughes et al., 2016). For more fully developed ideas, see Chapter 5.

Reflection

We continue to explore the implications of cultural competency in school counseling in order to take action. If you are in a higher education setting, consider these questions related to building a comprehensive developmental school counseling program:

1   What impact did your upbringing in school have on your desire to be a school counselor?

   a   If these experiences were positive, what in particular stands out to you?
   b   If these experiences were less positive, what compels you to still pursue a career within the school counseling profession, and what can you do differently?

2   What might school counseling programs look like if the staff had greater racial and cultural inclusiveness?

   a   How will increased inclusivity impact the students we serve?
   b   How might increased inclusivity advance learning among school counselors of a dominant culture?

3   What impact does the race and/or culture of the school counselor have on these programs?
4   How might you use your racial and cultural assets as a social justice champion in school settings?
5   How might our own development impact our work with minoritized students?

In the following activity, the authors expound on current and emerging concepts in the field of counseling at the intersection of cultural competency, social justice, and decolonization. Extend your learning using this activity in group or paired work.

Activity

In addition to our Pre-K-12 experiences, we also have educational experiences in our master's program that shed light on how we understand our own racial background and how we may engage others in contextualizing race. Below is an artifact in the form of a journal reflection assignment associated with the best-selling multicultural counseling textbook written by Sue et al. (2022), which is in its ninth edition! The excerpt written by Sam when he was in his master's program is presented first. Next, we provide an opportunity for the reader to pause and react to this entry as if they were the professor. Following this, we present the professor's actual response to the journal reflection.

Counselor Education Master's Program Multicultural Counseling Course Reflection Excerpt (Author's response to former school counseling professor's assignment, March 14, 2000)

In class, we reviewed two models about race. I find the White Identity Developmental model interesting and a good sign that there are attempts the professionals in our society are making to become well-rounded or culturally unbiased when considering educating others. When reviewing the African American model discussed by Cross, there were four stages – pre-encounter, encounter, immersion/emersion, and internalization – that were presented. According to this model, I see myself in the last stage at this point in my life. The internalization stages seem to be where I am because I see good and bad in both cultures, however, I believe I feel most comfortable in my own culture and around my own people. I feel this way because my family primarily consists of my culture and ethnic group, and I feel most comfortable around my family. The last stage is one that I believe I most identify with because it is not necessary for me to be immersed in my culture. This is probably not by choice but simply a reality. The atmosphere I work in and attend to when furthering my education is primarily dominated by the dominant culture of our society. I feel comfortable but would readily accept a change in the dynamics if and when this takes place.

We also discussed the Minority Identity Development Model. This model supposedly applies to all minorities. In this model, there were five stages – conformity, dissonance, resistance and immersion, introspection, and integrative awareness. According to this model, I fit in the intro-spection stages as well as the integrative awareness stages. At times I am concerned with a basis for self-appreciation and believe everyone should share this feeling at times. I am concerned with the nature of inequality and have a concern with an ethnocentric basis for judging others. In addition to this stage, I could fit into the integrative stages as well because I am self-appreciating and group-appreciating. Further, my attitude towards others in the dominant group is they should have a self-appreciation towards themselves as well. What I learned from all of this information that will help me in my counseling profession is that I should help clients to acknowledge their self-deprecating views and correct them if they are part of their impasse in their motivation for seeking counseling. This is probably easier said than done.

Pause for a moment. If you were the reviewer of this journal entry, what are your present reactions that would influence how you would respond? We provide a space for you to explore things you might say if you were the professor. Next, find the actual response Sam received from his professor.

School Counseling Professor's Response to the Author

"Sounds like you feel that these models are important" and useful for practitioners who desire to be well-rounded and "culturally unbiased." You see yourself in the last stage of Cross's theory and I'm wondering how so? What specific attitudes, behaviors, and beliefs do you have that demonstrate the stages chosen? You mentioned feeling most comfortable "in my own culture" and "my own family" – this is because of what in particular? You share that you feel it is not necessary to be immersed in your one culture and that it's not a choice but a "reality." Is this a reality for everyone? You also share that you are comfortable with members of the "dominant culture." How were you able to achieve this level of comfort you currently possess? Regarding the Minority Identity Development Model, you seem skeptical that this model applies to all minorities when you say that it "supposedly" applies to all with minority status. You seem less confident that this model applies and I'm wondering why you think this is the case. You also say that you desire everyone to be at a stage where they can appreciate themselves. At the same time, you seem concerned about inequality and the use of an "ethnocentric basis" for judging and categorizing others. Regardless, you have learned to appreciate yourself, your group, and others from different groups. How have you been able to achieve this stage? Lastly, you desire to help others reach a point where they can appreciate themselves and their cultural group, correct their self-deprecating views, and flourish. How will you do this if you make this happen in your career, and what will it look like?

In support of readers' journey and growth, we have provided both student and professor accounts during one of the author's thoughts at a critical stage in his school counseling program. The purpose is to gain a better understanding of the ongoing need for school counselors to engage in this type of introspective and reflection. This process has different starting points for each person, but it can be done.

Summary

The development of a social justice advocate is possibly a more intro-spective process heavily influenced by the experiences lived by the coun-selor. Theoretically speaking, the process starts initially as internal and focused on the individual's development. This introspection leads to ex-ternal foci that spur ongoing growth and development. Cyclical in nature, counselors continuously self-reflect to better serve their clients/students.

Key Takeaways

1 Structural inequities do impact student achievement.
2 When evaluating students, we can view their strengths using a culturally sustaining lens.
3 Social justice identity is developed over time.

Chapter Application

1 Examine the racial, ethnic, and socio-cultural demographics of school districts. What role can you play in addressing any inequities that surface?
2 Reflect on a local school district case that you can find in the newspaper that involves a race-related situation. Examine the case using your unique racial identity and racial attitudes.
3 Take a look at the ASCA position statements, which are guiding statements written to provide examples for counselors to take action. When thinking about students across the racial spectrum, which ones

are particularly relevant? For those position statements that are exclusionary (i.e., fail to be inclusive), generate some ideas to make them more straightforward at ensuring representation is evident.

4 Critically examine your school counseling program. In what ways are the tenets of the theories presented integrated into your program? In what ways are they not?

Reference List

American School Counselor Association. (2021). ASCA research report: State of the profession 2020. https://www.schoolcounselor.org/getmedia/bb23299b678d-4bce-8863-cfcb55f7df87/2020-State-of-theProfession.pdf

Arredondo, P. (1999). Multicultural counseling competencies as tools to address oppression and racism. *Journal of Counseling & Development, 77*(1), 102–108.

Auxier, C. R., Hughes, F. R., & Kline, W. B. (2003). Identity development in counselors-in-training. *Counselor Education and Supervision, 43*(1), 25–38.

Bell, D. A. (1994). *Confronting authority: Reflections of an ardent protester.* Boston: Beacon Press.

Boykin, A. W. (1986). The triple quandary and the schooling of Afro-American children. In U. Neisser (Ed.), *The school achievement of minority children* (pp. 57–92). Hillsdale, NJ: Lawrence Erlbaum.

Brott, P. E., & Myers, J. E. (1999). Development of professional school counselor identity. *Professional School Counseling, 2*(5), 339–348.

Burgess, D., Prescod, D. J., Bryan, J., & Chatters, S. (2021). Raising youth critical consciousness: Exploring critical race pedagogy as a framework for anti-racist programming. *Journal of School Counseling, 19*(34), n34.

Caldwell, J. C., & Vera, E. M. (2010). Critical incidents in counseling psychology professionals' and trainees' social justice orientation development. *Training and Education in Professional Psychology, 4*(3), 163–176. doi:10. 1037/a0019093

Constantine, M. G., Hage, S. M., Kindaichi, M. M., & Bryant, R. M. (2007). Social justice and multicultural issues: Implications for the practice and training of counselors and counseling psychologists. *Journal of Counseling & Development, 85*(1), 24–29.

Counts, G. S. (1932). *Dare the school build a new social order?.* Carbondale: Southern Illinois University Press.

DayVines, N. L., Brodar, J. R., Hicks, D., Fernandez-Korto, E. B., Garcia, C., & Jones, K. (2022). An investigation of the relationship between school counselor trainees' broaching behavior and their racial identity attitudes. *Journal of Counseling & Development, 100*(1), 3–13.

Field, J. E., & Baker, S. (2004). Defining and examining school counselor advocacy. *Professional School Counseling, 8,* 56–63.

Friere, P. (1968). *Pedagogy of the oppressed.* New York: Continuum.

Friere, P. (2000). Teaching the cultural conflicts. *Words in the Wilderness: Critical Literacy in the Borderlands, 181.*

Gibson, D. M., Dollarhide, C. T., & Moss, J. M. (2010). Professional identity development: A grounded theory of transformational tasks of new counselors. *Counselor Education and Supervision, 50*(1), 21–38.

Gorski, P. C. (2009). What we're teaching teachers: An analysis of multicultural teacher education coursework syllabi. *Teaching and Teacher Education, 25*(2), 309–318.

Hackman, H. W. (2005). Five essential components for social justice education. *Equity & Excellence in Education, 38*(2), 103–109.

Harro, B. (2010a). The cycle of socialization. In M. Adams, W. J. Blumenfeld, C. Casteneda, H. W. Hackman, M. L. Peters, and X. Zuniga (Eds.), *Readings for Diversity and Social Justice* (2nd ed., pp. 45–51). New York, NY: Routledge.

Harro, B. (2010b). The cycle of liberation. In M. Adams, W. J. Blumenfeld, C. Casteneda, H. W. Hackman, M. L. Peters, and X. Zuniga (Eds.), *Readings for Diversity and Social Justice* (2nd ed., pp. 52–58). New York, NY: Routledge.

Holcomb-McCoy, C. (2022). *School counseling to close opportunity gaps: A social justice and antiracist framework for success.* Corwin Press.

Hughes, D. L., Watford, J. A., & Del Toro, J. (2016). A transactional/ecological perspective on ethnic–racial identity, socialization, and discrimination. *Advances in Child Development and Behavior, 51*, 1–41.

Ieva, K. P., Steen, S., & Beasley, J. J. (2022). Preparing school counselors for social justice group counseling: Examining, power, privilege, and intersectionality. *Counselor Education and Supervision.*

Jones, C. T., & Galdy, G. R. (2022). African Americans: Substance use, grief, and loss. *Grief Work in Addictions Counseling*, 99–122.

Lugg, C. A., & Shoho, A. R. (2006). Dare public school administrators build a new social order? Social justice and the possibly perilous politics of educational leadership. *Journal of Educational Administration, 44*(3), 196–208.

Mayes, R. D., Edirmanasinghe, N., Ieva, K., & Washington, A. R. (2022, December). Liberatory school counseling practices to promote freedom dreaming for Black youth. In *Frontiers in Education* (Vol. 7, p. 966). Frontiers.

McAuliffe, G., Danner, M., Grothaus, T., & Doyle, L. (2008). Social inequality and social justice. *Culturally Alert Counseling: A Comprehensive Introduction*, 45–83.

McMahan, E. H., Singh, A. A., Urbano, A., & Haston, M. (2010). The personal is political: School counselors' use of self in social justice advocacy work. *Journal of School Counseling, 8*(18), n18.

McFarland, J., Hussar, B., Wang, X., Zhang, J., Wang, K., Rathbun, A.,... & Mann, F. B. (2018). The Condition of Education 2018. NCES 2018-144. *National Center for Education Statistics.*

Murrell Jr, P. C. (2006). Toward social justice in urban education: A model of collaborative cultural inquiry in urban schools. *Equity & Excellence in Education, 39*(1), 81–90.

Prosek, E. A., & Hurt, K. M. (2014). Measuring professional identity development among counselor trainees. *Counselor Education and Supervision, 53*(4), 284–293.

Ratts, M. J., Singh, A. A., Nassar-McMillan, S., Butler, S. K., & McCullough, J. R. (2016). Multicultural and social justice counseling competencies: Guidelines for the counseling profession. *Journal of Multicultural Counseling and Development, 44*(1), 28–48.

Sue, D. W., Sue, D., Neville, H. A., & Smith, L. (2022). *Counseling the culturally diverse: Theory and practice.* John Wiley & Sons.

Singh, A. A., Urbano, A., Haston, M., & McMahon, E. (2010). School counselors' strategies for social justice change: A grounded theory of what works in the real world. *Professional School Counseling, 13*(3), 135–145. Retrieved from http://www.jstor.org/stable/42732887

Vera, E. M., & Speight, S. L. (2003). Multicultural competence, social justice, and counseling psychology: Expanding our roles. *The Counseling Psychologist, 31*(3), 253–272.

Part II

Reimagining Equity within the School Counseling Profession

Chapter 5

Community-Driven, Evidence-Based Comprehensive School Counseling Programs and Leadership

Key Terms (See Chapter 1)
Coordination, Critical Consciousness, Family Engagement

Author Narrative: Sam Steen

My first job as an elementary school counselor in Williamsburg, Virginia, prepared me to handle the unknown. Because I applied on a whim while still completing my counseling degree, I was not fully prepared for this job. Despite my counselor training program, I had no idea of the wide variety of experiences that I would encounter in a school setting. The rapid daily pace and strikingly short school year drowned me. I recall, during internship supervision, sharing stories about not knowing the lingo and multiple acronyms used by school staff, drastic developmental differences between kindergartners and first graders, and the impact of seemingly trivial things on different aspects of the school. Major issues that came up daily would fizzle out quicker than I suspected. This taught me how to be patient, even amid crises or other less-critical issues that seemed so significant at the time.

The second job I obtained was a full-time position, and I was a newly minted professional school counselor for 850 pre-K-3rd graders in Manassas Park, Virginia. My rigorous internship had fully prepared me for this position, which was equally exciting and demanding. From previous experience, I was aware of how simple things that occurred in one part of the school (e.g., classrooms, recess area, cafeteria, bus stop) or in a student's household, neighborhood, or broader community could impact the entire school community. A *systems thinking* perspective emerged for me during this time and it continues to this day. The primer I received on the ASCA National Model before graduating from my master's program had some influence, as there was an emphasis on seeing the school as a system and approaching the work comprehensively and developmentally appropriate for the students. During my early career, the National Model was promoted

DOI: 10.4324/9781003226253-7

as the most important tool to meet the needs of all students. However, in my actual work, I was often left wondering, "what about families, teachers, bus drivers, and the siblings of these students?" Although this model was important, it was not complex enough to help me conceptualize how to employ programs and interventions that could meet the community's needs.

This job influenced me to return to school to gain additional training and education. I was accepted to a PhD program where I developed the beginning stages of a professional identity that allowed me to apply research and scholarship to the experiences I was encountering at work every day. Obtaining a PhD in school counseling and education is not a prerequisite to building a data-driven, evidence-based, comprehensive developmental school counseling program; however, this additional education and professional development helped me understand the rationale for basing our work specifically on the communities being served. These communities (i.e., our communities) have strengths and assets that can inform models to ensure the research emerging from these models are based on culturally sustaining school counseling practice. I continue today as a counselor educator who aims to produce research and scholarship based on the articulated needs and desires of the school communities I hope to help flourish and thrive.

Content

History of the School Counseling Profession

The National Defense Education Act (NDEA) of 1958 was instituted to broaden school counseling training in both higher education and district settings around the country (Herr, 2001). Secondary school counselors guided students' trajectories into university or employment upon graduation. The legislation allocated millions of federal dollars for vocational testing systems, the creation of school counseling programs at the elementary level, professional development, and evaluation of student services and counseling processes that align with school instruction. The Reagan Administration commissioned the *Nation at Risk* report (1983), which stoked the fire of dissatisfied education stakeholders, decision-makers, and funders who compared American students with their counterparts around the world. Almost 25 years after the NDEA passed, convoluted definitions of school counseling and uneven investments in school accountability yielded mixed results.

With the passing of the Carl D. Perkins Education Act (Perkins Act of 1984), the field yet again shifted to focus on professional competencies and student outcomes related to college entrance, career readiness, and student assessment of career needs (Friedel, 2006). This landmark legislation legitimized the term "*school counseling program*" (Herr, 2001, p. 241) and added new dimensions to school counseling programs by mandating that schools help students accomplish the following objectives:

1 Acquire self-assessment, career planning, decision-making, and employability skills;
2 Make the transition from education and training to work;
3 Maintain marketability of job skills in established occupations;
4 Develop new skills to move away from declining occupational fields and enter new and emerging fields in high-technology areas and fields experiencing skill shortages;
5 Develop mid-career job search skills and clarify career goals; and
6 Obtain and use information on financial assistance for postsecondary and vocational education and job training (Title III, Section 521, [4]).

As you read the different objectives above take a moment to consider the following questions. Can you name one or two objectives that are still very much observed in schools today? Can you name one or two objectives that are not showing up? What is missing from these objectives that you have observed as important and that could be mandated? How different might these objectives read if we added more inclusive language that reflects all students?

In coordination with the recent Every Student Succeeds Act (2015), the Perkins Act defines many of the responsibilities and priorities of school counselors. Questions remain about whether excessively centering the areas of math, science, and technology creates systemic inequities for under-resourced schools and students who have been tracked out of rigorous learning opportunities in middle and secondary school (e.g., magnet, Advanced Placement, International Baccalaureate, or honors classes). The work of school counselors is multifaceted and dependent on the needs, strengths, composition, and mission of their distinct school community. This complexity reflects opportunity *and* the importance of critical reflection on ways to thrive personally and professionally as a school counselor. The role of a school counselor must be situated within the context of social justice advocacy for students, families, school communities, and the profession overall. This positionality, or equity and access, for all students (Atkins & Oglesby, 2018) brings clarity, space to reflect, and urgency to advocate collectively.

The School Counselor's Evolving Responsibilities, Contextual Demands, and Political Mandates

School counseling, similarly, became more prevalent as the education field grappled with the benefits of vocational and industrial training nearly 75 years ago. The American-Soviet Space Race led to the Sputnik launch and subsequent political calls for drastic reforms in our schools (Herr, 2001). Several nascent questions echoed in the halls of power:

a   What factors and conditions caused American students to fall behind in science and math?
b   Which students deserved targeted support to increase their potential to succeed in college at the highest levels?
c   With limited school resources, how might schools evaluate student competency for university and career performance in advantageous fields?

School Counselor Roles

Throughout the school counseling profession's brief history, the debate over the roles of school counselors has been prominent. It is not always readily evident what activities are considered appropriate and inappropriate for school counselors. Table 5.1 was created by ASCA to offer specificity on the continuum of roles and activities as well as the nuances evident in a school setting. Even if clearly stated, to what extent are these activities feasible or realistic? What stands out as noteworthy? What areas need improvement? To what extent do these roles consider race, class, and gender as part of conceptualizing how to work in a culturally sustaining manner?

In Table 5.1, there is a clear lack of discussion of race, class, gender, and other personal characteristics that inform one's perspective on these activities. If we suspect this document found on the ASCA website was written to apply to *all* students, then we might be upholding our blinders to white supremacy. When reviewing these recommendations it is debatable the extent to which school counselors have a say in not doing certain activities needing attention in a school. Let's review a few of these appropriate and inappropriate school counselor roles using a multicultural lens.

For example, are absences related to a particular religious practice? Or, are there any patterns in school attendance that show up? Are there issues regarding transportation? What will it take to learn more about what's being observed? We must give all students and families the benefit of the doubt and create inclusive and equitable environments that will necessitate an ongoing examination of policies, procedures, and practices.

At times the duties that a school needs you to perform and those that are discussed as part of your training program might not always align. For instance, school counseling leaders within ASCA (see position statement on the ASCA website The School Counselor and Discipline) discourage school counselors from supervising and/or functioning as a disciplinarian within classrooms or common areas. This duty sounds like child care,

Table 5.1 **Appropriate vs Inappropriate School Counseling Activities**

Appropriate Activities for SCs	Inappropriate Activities for SCs
Advisement and appraisal for academic planning	Building the master schedule
Orientation, coordination, and academic advising for new students	
Interpreting cognitive, aptitude, and achievement tests	Proctoring school standardized tests (e.g., end of course, Advanced Placement, Scholastic Aptitude Test)
Providing counseling to students who are tardy or absent	Enforcing attendance policies
Providing counseling to students who have disciplinary problems	Giving consequences for discipline issues
Providing short-term individual and small-group counseling services to students	Counseling students with no end date
Consulting with teachers to schedule and present school counseling curriculum lessons based on developmental needs and needs identified through data	Teacher evaluation and observations
Interpreting student records	Maintaining student records
Analyzing grade-point averages in relationship to achievement	Computing grade-point averages
Consulting with teachers about building classroom connections, effective classroom management, and the role of noncognitive factors in student success	Supervising classrooms or common areas
Protecting student records and information per state and federal regulations	Keeping clerical records
Consulting with the school principal to identify and resolve student issues, needs, and problems	Assisting with duties in the principal's office
Advocating for students at individual education plan meetings, student study teams, and school attendance review boards, as necessary	Coordinating school-wide individual education plans, 504 plans, student study teams, response to intervention plans, MTSS, and school attendance review boards
Analyzing disaggregated school-wide and school counseling program data	Serving as a data entry clerk

babysitting, or administrative activity. The argument against engaging in supervising students in the classroom or during recess is that you could be spending time doing more productive things. However, anytime we can work directly with students offers an opportunity for school counselors to build solid relationships with students while spending time monitoring, engaging, and interacting with them outside of the classroom or the counseling office. It is important to note that operating as a school/student disciplinarian can be counterproductive; however, there will be times when you are connecting with students and problematic behaviors unfold. You will need to discuss and negotiate the role you will take concerning discipline, while also maintaining your focus on advocating that students are treated fairly and equitably. This does not apply only to racially minoritized children and adolescents; however, the data is also clear that Black males and females in particular are treated egregiously when others are afforded leniency when similar issues are displayed. The role of a school counselor can be delicate, but expanding the potential to serve more students stimulates creativity toward equity and access in schools. More attention will be given to applying the roles and functions of school counselors throughout this text.

Models and School Counseling

According to O'Neil and Denke (2016), a model is an abstract depiction of a process based on what is known and how this information or knowledge is applied in various situations and contexts. In school counseling textbooks and related published articles, the ASCA National Model for School Counseling Programs is one model that is comprehensive, developmental, and data-driven, or based on evidence that is emerging. ASCA recommends that the student-to-school-counselor ratio be 250 to 1, which confirms the impact of school counselors. It is important for school counselors to develop a model for their students and families based on the unique needs of the students and families within the community. As a result, the model cannot truly be created without input from students, their caretakers, and other members of the community. Particular attention is needed for Black students and families to ensure their brilliance is highlighted and celebrated. Exploring strengths and assets challenges the historical and systemic racism within educational systems that must be eradicated. Members of the community can share their current perspectives and suggestions for healing. One way to oppose oppressive educational environments is to offer comprehensive, developmental school counseling programs that are community-driven, with information coming from the students, families, and school staff stakeholders. The data (e.g., qualitative, quantitative, and the integration of these data) helps to articulate said needs. A skilled and savvy school counselor works in concert with the school community to ensure that the focus is on the students and their families. Fostering relationships is an essential aspect of a school counselor's role. School counselors integrate social justice and empowerment when they actively commit to building school-family-community partnerships (Bryan & Henry, 2012). Below we briefly discuss some common school counseling models: the ASCA National Model; Ecological

Model; Transforming School Counselor Initiative; and National Office School Counseling Advocacy.

American School Counseling Association

The auspicious timing of the American School Counseling Association (ASCA) National Model should be noted. Prior to 2000, comprehensive models had been emerging sporadically across the U.S. Before the ASCA National Model's first edition was released in 1998, comprehensive developmental and school-based models provided the various structures that have been applied within public schools. One early criticism of the ASCA National Model was its motto suggesting that *all* students would benefit from school counselors applying this framework, but how is this truly possible? In other words, can one model be applied to every student within the U.S.? The early version of the model, and arguably subsequent versions, were made up of a small group of well-intentioned individuals who failed to offer the true lived experiences and needs of Black students who might not so easily align with the dominant White and Eurocentric culture. Despite the ASCA National Model's limitations, it has existed for nearly 25 years and offers a popular and consistent manner in which to build a school counseling program. ASCA suggests that advising counselors for academic planning orientation, coordination, and academic advising for new students are appropriate activities. ASCA also believes that interpreting cognitive, aptitude, and achievement tests are appropriate activities to participate in as well. However, The ASCA National Model (American School Counselor Association, 2019) is now in its fourth edition and offers a clear, concise manner for easy replication. The ASCA National Model consists of four components: 1) Define, 2) Manage, 3) Deliver, and 4) Assess.

Activity

In your own words, provide definitions for each of the four ASCA National Model components below. In addition to a definition, give an example or illustration of each component. Next, visit the ASCA website, where you can find an executive summary. This summary can be used to clarify the intentions of the ASCA National Model.

Definitions for:

Define
Manage
Deliver
Assess

Examples and illustrations of:

Define
Manage
Deliver
Assess

Consider what you wrote in comparison to what is described in the ASCA executive summary. What more do you need to learn in the future? What are some recommendations that you have for the ASCA leaders, to modify the ASCA National Model based on your own personal and professional perspectives? What about ideas to ensure the model functions as a tool that fosters equity and inclusive excellence?

Ecological Model

Outside of school counseling, educators and researchers from various helping professions realize the importance of seeing students and families within their community contexts. The students within the school environment are heavily influenced by forces within and outside the school. The Ecological Model allows school counselors to situate their schools within the different levels of society, spanning from the individual to the family, the community, and beyond. The ecological model provides a framework that can be applied in practice and research.

For example, an ecological framework offers opportunities for advocacy in school systems to help overcome barriers and encourage resistance when experiencing inequitable spaces. An ecological model is timely, specific, and well-suited to attending to school and community-related needs. To illustrate a unique example, a social-ecological model for preventing violence was found. It recognizes factors – such as individual, relationship, community, and societal – and these factors are interwoven in complex ways that overlap with one another, yet explicit language and terminology about race are missing.

Ecological school counseling (ESC) is a paradigm that conceptualizes schools as ecosystems, operating under systemic principles such as interactional causality, interconnectedness, and dynamic balance. The role of the school counselor is to understand and work with students within and across their multiple ecosystems and to create healthier systems in which students can learn and grow. School counselors working from this perspective advocate for systemic change and help students develop the awareness and skills to be successful in a variety of their ecosystems, including school. To meet this goal, ecological school counselors must work directly with students as well as collaborate with stakeholders across ecosystems. The vital duties of the ecological school counselor include identifying the feedback that is signaling distress, identifying ecological factors that are likely contributing to the issue, and initiating the change process across multiple levels to facilitate the systems' changing themselves.

Transforming School Counseling Initiative

Another model that has had a major influence on school counselor programs across the nation is a result of the Education Trust's (Ed Trust) herculean efforts to close achievement gaps and offer opportunities for students no matter where they come from or where they currently reside. The Transforming School Counseling Initiative (TSCI) believes the most important outcome is academic development. The TSCI most closely relates to a social justice framework, as it squarely fosters equity-focused advocacy initiatives. The TSCI received major funding from the DeWitt Wallace Foundation to transform school counselor education programs and to ensure the preparation they were receiving would help them be prepared to help students succeed in school despite numerous racial and ethnic barriers.

Equity-focused research studies were funded by TSCI and while this initiative was short-lived, the benefits from this funding and the ongoing mission of the Ed Trust have continued to offer compelling evidence to create programs that offer time, support, and resources needed for all students to win in schools. For instance, recently, the Ed Trust commissioned a study outlining gaps in Black and Latine students either enrolling in or having access to AP STEM-related courses in high school. Rather than simply reiterating the issues, gaps, and inequities, the Ed Trust provided the following strategies to impact policy and its implications for school counseling practice. The different strategies include but are not limited to: a) setting clear, measurable goals for advancing access to and success in advanced coursework, and b) committing to publicly measuring state and district progress toward those goals.

Additionally, the Ed Trust suggests that data can be used to identify protective factors to barriers and targeted suggestions that could foster resiliency for Black and Latine students who have been discouraged or prevented from enrolling in advanced courses. The Ed Trust recognizes the necessity of providing the financial resources needed so more students can access AP STEM courses, especially those attending schools in low-income communities. For racially minoritized schools, it will necessitate school counselors posturing as advocates and less as gatekeepers to increase enrollment within AP STEM courses and the support needed to be successful.

Ultimately, schools must expand eligibility and increase access for Black and Latine students to have a fair chance to enroll in advanced coursework. School counselors can lead these efforts.

Most of the models above consistently fail to intentionally use the cultural context of racial and ethnic minoritized families. In particular, Black students and their families have not been centered in these aforementioned models. However, the following models within educational research, counseling, and school counseling respectively offer important aspects to consider as equity and access become priorities for school counselors desiring to center the needs of students from the myriad of backgrounds that intersect with Black culture and Black people.

Halgunseth Model on Family-School Partnerships

Family engagement represents a two-way, reciprocal strengths-based partnership among schools, families, teachers, and education communities that supports children's environmental growth (Halgunseth et al., 2009). This partnership is distinct from conventional parent involvement, which merely focuses on what parents are doing in schools instead of engagement guided by the family's many seen and unseen contributions, integral relationships, and shared goals.

García Coll et al. (1996)'s Integrative Model for the Study of Developmental Competencies in Minority Children

Historical models of research for African American/Black children and their families were established on deficiency (García Coll et al., 1996). Black parents and families were often blamed for their children's lack of Eurocentric cultural norms, and these students were often compared to a white standard. Models could move away from blaming families and comparing Black children with their White peers. But an intentional effort will need to be made to overcome the misconception that Black children, no matter their economic or societal position, hold deficits (Ladson-Billings, 2000).

Models within education can infuse race and social class and the unique aspects of Black children's school experiences to build on the fact that race has been found to be of theoretical significance in relationships for Black children and families (Lareau & Horvat, 1999). Moving beyond the acceptance that Black culture is legitimate within classrooms and seeing Black children as having powerful rather than oppositional or deviant characteristics from White mainstream culture will take a concerted effort. In the original Integrative Model of Child Development, children's characteristics influence their environments and these factors influence important developmental outcomes (García Coll et al., 1996). To illustrate, Blackness for African Americans within the U.S. is said to perform three functions in everyday life:

• Defending the individual from the negative psychological stress of living in a racist society;
• Providing a sense of purpose, affiliation, and meaning; and
• Providing psychological mechanisms that facilitate social interaction with non-African-American people, situations, and cultures (Cross, 1991).

While it would be inappropriate to assume these functions apply to every African American/Black person in this country, it does hold true for many folks today. More times than not, school policies and procedures that support deficit narratives aim to keep systems and institutions based on White cultural standards and norms. However, celebrating Blackness and all aspects of life through this lens is inclusive of all races and cultures.

The Multidimensional Model of Broaching Behavior

Two decades ago, Day-Vines et al. (2007) developed the continuum of broaching behavior model in an effort to enumerate dispositions and language that counselors can use to discuss their racial, ethnic, and cultural (REC) concerns with clients. The different categories were labeled avoidant, isolating, continuing/incongruent, integrated/congruent, and infusing. Broaching is defined, in this case, as a school counselor's deliberate and intentional attempts to shed light on and talk about REC concerns that may impact the students' presenting issues. In addition to either initiating or responding to REC content that comes up during the counseling interactions, counselors who use effective broaching behavior and skills apply this understanding of the student's sociocultural and sociopolitical narratives (e.g., school climate, academic achievement) into meaningful counseling practice. This model is very detailed and the research evidence demonstrates improvements in problem-solving, client empowerment, and fostering of resilience. On the other hand, if REC concerns are overlooked, disregarded, or discouraged, the perpetuation of the dominant culture remains (Day-Vines et al., 2020).

The role and function of school counselors have been a frequent topic in educational literature (Borders & Drury, 1992; Burnham & Jackson, 2000; Gysbers & Henderson, 2001; House & Hayes, 2002; NOSCA, 2011), with ongoing debates about what the job entails and how the work should be organized. While there is general agreement among educators, parents, and school boards to have counselors in public schools, there is a wide range of opinions about what counselors should be doing to help students. Some of the debate has been in response to contextual factors such as No Child Left

Behind (No Child Left Behind Act [NCLB], 2002) and the current Reach Higher Initiative (Hatch & Owen, 2015). Models can be made to address discrepancies between the expectations of administrators and school counselors (Amatea & Clark, 2005; Cole, 1991; Perusse et al., 2004), but which model or models should be the focus of these school counseling efforts?

A successful school counseling (SC) model should provide guidance in continuously matching students with effective services. An effective SC model that is intentional at celebrating Blackness should focus on the true identity of the students and their families. Schools are complex systems, and an effective SC model ideally provides guidance about how school counselors can collaborate with other professionals to support Black students and the wider school community.

Critiquing Models within the School Counseling Context

Models are defined as frameworks that either are based on theory or based on practice. Models provide a sketch of important components that are necessary to build an intervention or program. Models for school counselors are often so specialized that other educators or stakeholders may be unfamiliar with the goals, objectives, and purposes of the particular model.

These models have systematically failed to include Black children and Black culture in the goals, objectives, and purposes. The current school climate necessitates that the race and culture of the students are infused into these models. Models used within school counseling should be guides that have flexibility built in, acknowledging and fostering the great strength of racially blended communities. In addition to broadening the application of these models, new and creative models that are designed for Black children are needed. For example, Byrd and colleagues created a small-group intervention "reading woke" as a form of academic and social-emotional emancipatory learning while fostering resiliency, strength, and creativity in Black children. This program will produce a model in which further study is warranted for establishing a myriad of strategies that highlight the strengths of Black students and their families. Byrd and colleagues also use antiracist practices to offer small-group opportunities for young Black girls to find a homeplace in schools while being unapologetically Black (Byrd et al., 2022).

Developing Models

Ideas to create models can emerge out of necessity or due to certain preferences (O'Neil & Denke, 2016). A model is used to ensure consistency in program delivery and offers guidance on important elements that are established from the onset of the programmatic efforts. Certain encounters stimulate ideas for what areas to focus on. The main purpose the model is created for will give you a sense of what it should be called or what it stands for. Outlining a cursory plan is an effective initial step in developing the "what" and "why," Following this brainstorming, it is important to generate clear goal(s) and clear objectives. However, we believe that the purpose, goal(s), and objectives cannot be made in isolation, and school counselors will need to be quite active in seeking input and support from the individual and communities (e.g., students, caretakers, teachers, and administrators) being served. School counselors committed to equity work recognize the vast amount of knowledge and skill that collaborating with others provides. Students, caretakers, teachers, and administrators all have unique perspectives, experiences, motivations, and desired outcomes that can be drawn upon when creating and applying models within the school counseling program.

Interdisciplinary Approaches and Comprehensive School Counseling Programs

Now more than ever, it is critical for school counselors working to foster equitable school environments for Black and Brown students to take an interdisciplinary approach. Interdisciplinary in this case is defined as a mixture and blend of areas of expertise within education. For instance, school counselors' background is partially based on psychology, counseling, mental health, and education. Teachers' knowledge and background in many cases include learning, instruction, pedagogy, and education. School administrators' foundations include learning, instruction, pedagogy, leadership, financial and facilities management, and so forth. This interdisciplinary lens can also work to intentionally include families, caretakers, other mental health professionals, community advocates, and cultural brokers to inform decisions that will impact the overall comprehensive school counseling program. The goal is to invite members within the community to have a platform to provide input.

Oftentimes school districts in large urban and suburban areas require school counselors to create data-driven, evidenced-based comprehensive developmental school counseling programs. Such a program cannot be successful or sustainable if driven only by data. Data-driven essentially means formally using facts, statistics, and relevant information to establish goals and objectives. Data-driven will need to also include informal sources, anecdotal narratives, and one's own observations to build a foundation upon which to provide areas to focus on and target. Data-driven-only is not sustainable unless you include both formal and informal data sources. Evidence-based will more fully capture counseling, programs, interventions, and systemic undertakings that are used to meet the needs of students, families, and school community members.

Critical Consciousness and Critical Political Standpoint

Educators and school counselors must advocate for others despite any difficulties that might be encountered. The students and families navigate highly oppressive environments within and outside of schools. School counselors can expose inequities and offer solutions by facilitating programs that provide opportunities for Black students to demonstrate their excellence. Critical consciousness is knowing about racialized paradigms and frameworks and the systemic racism some face based on race and race-related factors (Burgess et al., 2021).

Critical consciousness is a viable framework for school counselors who center the voices and lived experiences of Black children and families. To engage in this work, school counselors cannot be passive, but must actively know that the decisions they make are political statements. School counselors can offer space for students to voice their opinions. Studies have shown that the more youth reported talking about race and racism when they are within their homes, the more they vocalized social justice values such as equal treatment for social groups (Bañales et al., 2021). When school counselors confront systemic issues head-on there may be some consequences, and in some cases, these choices are physically and emotionally taxing. However, oppression affects both the oppressed and the oppressor; therefore, leading others to engage in challenging inequities offers greater chances of dismantling the anti-Blackness that is embedded within our schools and communities.

Using Evidence to Be More Inclusive

Interventions within these comprehensive programs often include individual counseling, group counseling, and developing these interventions within a racialized context is necessary. The challenge about evidence-based school counseling is that, historically, those who were pursuing research inquiry to discover the evidence were limited by those who held the power and privileges. In other words, not everyone had a seat at the table; therefore, only a few were selected to determine what evidence was important to pursue (e.g., quantitative), which players would be afforded the resources and outlets to produce this evidence, and which communities this evidence was provided for. School counseling leaders have made concerted efforts to ensure that school counselor practitioners and counselor educators alike were welcomed to engage in this fight for social justice and equity when it comes to evidence.

In fact, there is an Evidence-Based School Counseling Conference each year that was started by several key leaders in our field and co-founded by Dr. Carey Dimmitt and Dr. Brett Zymromski, whom Sam personally can say has had a major influence on his thinking as a researcher and practitioner-scholar. There is more work to be done, and areas for improvement include examining broader perspectives of "evidence-based" interventions, programs, models, and school counseling mechanisms. Simply put, should the goal of evidence-based models be to replicate and generalize findings from one community to another? Or, perhaps, should the goal be to provide evidence that works within the unique context in which the findings emerged? This dialog is currently underway with school counseling leaders across the nation.

Readiness to Develop a Community-Focused Comprehensive School Counseling Program Can Be Determined by One's Personal Barometer

Only the school counselors themselves can truly know whether or not they are ready to engage in these tough discussions about equity, access, and inclusive excellence. At this point, how would you describe some strategies to create and apply a community-focused and interdisciplinary approach to comprehensive school counseling programs? With this line of thinking are you able to include a nod towards critical consciousness and a critical political standpoint when developing a plan to help students and their families? It may help to think about a specific outcome that you desire. For instance, feel free to determine the project that you will employ and the data you will use to claim that it is evidence-based practice. Reflecting your readiness to develop a community-driven, evidence-based, comprehensive school counseling program is something that you will need to continually engage in.

Activity

In order to be intentional in infusing positive and inclusive frameworks, what do you believe is currently lacking in your counselor preparation program? Describe some topics that are missing that would strengthen your future work as a school counselor. Feel free to draw from your practicum/service-learning experiences, any class discussions, readings, or other interesting material. Next, consider this reflection of a budding school counselor who was a first-year school counselor at the time of this publication. This reflection is written as a letter from a first-year school counselor to a school counselor trainee.

Reflecting on Year 1

Dear school counselor trainee:

A saying often heard in education is, *"remember your why,"* referring to recalling why you decided to pursue a career in education. Students who may face the same challenges I once did during childhood have always been my "why." The first few years of my childhood were quite a roller coaster ride. By age eight, I had moved from the United Kingdom to Canada and then to the United States after my father passed away from leukemia. Like many traditional Ghanaian Christian families, the focus in our household was primarily on education and less on mental health or social-emotional needs. Respect for your elders is an essential value in Ghanaian culture, so I tried my best to do what I was told to avoid adding additional stress to my widowed mother's plate. However, the drastic life changes did take a toll on my emotions and made it difficult to maintain a positive attitude.

In addition to struggling with significant family changes, I also struggled with my identity. Many of my peers and I had shared identities when living in the Greater Toronto Area. I was surrounded by many immigrants, first-generation Canadians, West Africans, and other Black racialized individuals of color. Growing up in Virginia, I was clearly in the minority and much less privileged than my classmates. Even with African American peers, I quickly realized that there were traditions and customs specific to the Black-American experience that I, who identified as Ghanaian before anything, didn't relate to. Frequent bullying due to my weight while being self-conscious of my hair texture and skin color also led to a negative self-concept.

When things were rough, my high school counselor was one of the people I found solace with. She had a calm, kind spirit and was always encouraging. As the supporting counselor for our school's college readiness program, my mother and I often reached out to her for advice on the college transition process. While it may not seem as though there was anything spectacular about our relationship, to me it was everything. As a child, when you're having trouble understanding the world around you, sometimes an adult showing they care is enough to turn your day around, even if only for a few hours. I always knew that when I became a school counselor, I would try to project some of that positive energy and kindness I received from my school counselor toward my students, even during difficult days. While I am still developing my identity as a school counselor, I hope to be the source of peace for my students, just as my school counselor was for me.

A significant takeaway from my first year in the field is that progress is rarely drastic, immediate, and seldom linear. In my first year as a school counselor, I believed that I had to find solutions quickly, and they needed to be effective immediately. Reality hit when I began working with a student with a history of school refusal early in the school year. On many days this student would arrive at school and remain in the parking lot for hours. Whenever the student succeeded in leaving early or missing school, I brainstormed new ideas to increase their attendance. These included positive reinforcements, attendance groups, morning check-ins, and more.

These interventions would lead to increased attendance for a short period or none. Each time an intervention proved unsuccessful, I would feel defeated. It was not until learning more about the student's history that the obvious started to click for me. I was trying to solve an issue more significant than myself in weeks, which was unrealistic. I also realized that a pandemic and an interruption in traditional schooling had exacerbated a problem that had manifested for years. I had to accept that progress for each student will look different, and often, it will be slow. For this student, I found that progress could look like coming to school, checking in with a trusted adult, and making it through the first period. A more significant improvement could be staying until lunch. Going into my second year at school counseling, I am letting go of viewing recurring issues with my students as failures to be an effective counselor. Instead, I see them as opportunities to learn and collaborate with other educators on ways to support student concerns. Lack of progress or regression can also make for valuable data and shed light on improving one's counseling program.

When I first decided to become a school counselor, I had all these grand ideas for the type of counselor I wanted to be. I wanted to promote equity and be an advocate, a change agent. I wanted to be a role model for young Black girls in the same school district where I grew up. By the end of the first half of the school year, I found myself discouraged and developed the idea that my work within my school was not as impactful as it could be. I compared myself to other counselors receiving recognition in the community for their advocacy or social justice work. I thought I'd never get to their level of success. Looking back on my first year of school counseling, I was unnecessarily hard on myself. Success as a counselor is not measured by the number of awards received, articles written, or how many protests you attend. It is measured by how a counselor works to make their school environment safe and inclusive for all students. I think back to my first National School Counselor Week. I received several cards from my students expressing their appreciation for my work. Some of these cards came from students with whom I had only had brief conversations. Yet, the words they used to express their gratitude for school counselors let me know that the work my program was doing was not going unnoticed. In my second year as a school counselor, I am giving myself grace and room to develop my own identity as a counselor. I am embracing my mistakes, asking for help, and remaining open to feedback. Most importantly, I remember to stay positive and care for my mental health so I can continue providing my students with the support they deserve.

Sincerely,
Nadia A. Boateng (Bwah-tin), M.Ed.
Seventh-Grade School Counselor

After reading this letter, go back and examine the responses to the Activity prompts you wrote initially and compare areas in which you may have changed after finishing this chapter.

Summary

School counselors who are intentional about gaining an understanding of their students' and their families' unique perspectives within their communities will offer more credible, valid, and realistic outcomes.

School counselors must critique and upend conceptual frameworks that guide their influence of race and culture in their responsibilities (e.g., helping families decide the proper placement for their students, interpreting test results, and navigating school rules and norms). For example, using a lens that celebrates people and their race, class, gender, and so on, helps build strong partnerships with parents and families to find solutions to the underlying issues that could be linked to student absenteeism. Barriers could be examined to determine *if* they are external to the student, classroom, family, and/or within the community. School counselors also must be transparent and honest about challenging school and district policies that might set up systemic barriers for some students and perpetuate their attendance difficulties. Their strengths and assets must be invited – seen and recognized even – in order to tackle chronic issues proactively.

Key Takeaways

1 Understanding the uniqueness of your school's culture and aligning your program accordingly is a necessary practice for school counselors.
2 Developing an inclusive comprehensive school counseling program that meets the needs of all students and their families, teachers, and staff is essential.
3 Recognizing one's biases in order to be more inclusive with all aspects of diversity Remember, every counselor is not a White woman and every Black and Brown child does not need help.
4 Evidence-based school counseling is not the problem. Believing that there is only one version of evidence.

Chapter Application

1 Provide a narrative of an alternative school and how would you incorporate a Comprehensive School Counseling Program in this non-traditional setting.
2 Identify other models that might be appropriate in the communities that you anticipate working in.

3 Dimmit (2003) stated, "The question is, of course, whether academic success is the result of self-esteem developed in early interpersonal experience, or whether self-esteem (particularly academic self-esteem) follows academic success." Where do you stand in this argument and why? Further, what are the implications for a professional school counselor and/or their school counseling programs, depending on which side of the above argument you support?

4 What other health professions can you borrow from to create school-wide environments that are supportive of students from racially and culturally blended communities?

References

Amatea, E. S., & Clark, M. A. (2005). Changing schools, changing counselors: A qualitative study of school administrators' conceptions of the school counselor role. *Professional School Counseling, 9*(1), 2156759X0500900101.

American School Counselor Association. (2019). *The ASCA National Model: A framework for school counseling programs* (4th ed.). Alexandria, VA.

Atkins, R., & Oglesby, A. (2018). *Interrupting racism: Equity and social justice in school counseling.* Routledge.

Bañales, J., Hope, E. C., Rowley, S. J., & Cryer-Coupet, Q. R. (2021). Raising justice-minded youth: Parental ethnic-racial and political socialization and Black youth's critical consciousness. *Journal of Social Issues, 77*(4), 964–986.

Borders, L. D., & Drury, S. M. (1992). Comprehensive school counseling. *Counseling & Development, 70,* 487–498.

Bryan, J., & Henry, L. (2012). A model for building school–family–community partnerships: Principles and process. *Journal of Counseling & Development, 90*(4), 408–420.

Burgess, D., Prescod, D. J., Bryan, J., & Chatters, S. (2021). Raising youth critical consciousness: Exploring critical race pedagogy as a framework for anti-racist programming. *Journal of School Counseling, 19*(34), n34.

Burnham, J. J., & Jackson, C. M. (2000). School counselor roles: Discrepancies between actual practice and existing models. *Professional School Counseling, 4,* 41.

Byrd, J., Porter, C., Mayes, R., & Ahmadi, A. (2022) "(In)Visibility across educational spaces: Centering mental health & wellness for black girls & women", *Journal of African American Women and Girls in Education, 2*(2), 1–8. doi: 10.21423/jaawge-v2i2a125.

Cole, C. G. (1991). Counselors and administrators: A comparison of roles. *NASSP Bulletin, 75*(534), 5–13.

Cross Jr, W. E. (1991). *Shades of black: Diversity in African-American identity.* Temple University Press.

Day-Vines, N. L., Cluxton-Keller, F., Agorsor, C., Gubara, S., & Otabil, N. A. A. (2020). The multidimensional model of broaching behavior. *Journal of Counseling & Development, 98*(1), 107–118.

Day-Vines, N. L., Wood, S. M., Grothaus, T., Craigen, L., Holman, A., Dotson-Blake, K., & Douglass, M. J. (2007). Broaching the subjects of race, ethnicity, and culture during the counseling process. *Journal of Counseling & Development*, *85*(4), 401–409.

Dimmitt, C. (2003). Transforming school counseling practice through collaboration and the use of data: A study of academic failure in high school. *Professional School Counseling*, *6*, 340–349.

Friedel, J. M. (2006). *Children's efficacy beliefs and coping strategies in mathematics across the transition to middle school: The roles of perceived parent and teacher achievement goal emphases.* (Doctoral dissertation).

García Coll, C. G., Crnic, K., Lamberty, G., Wasik, B. H., Jenkins, R., García, H. V., & McAdoo, H. P. (1996). An integrative model for the study of developmental competencies in minority children. *Child Development*, *67*(5), 1891–1914. 10.1111/j.1467-8624.1996.tb01834.x

Gysbers, N. C., & Henderson, P. (2001). Comprehensive guidance and counseling programs: A rich history and a bright future. *Professional School Counseling*, *4*, 246.

Halgunseth, L., Peterson, A., Stark, D., & Moodie, S. (2009). Family engagement, diverse families, and early childhood education programs: An integrated review of the literature. *Young Children*, *64*(5), 56–58.

Hatch, T., & Owen, L. (2015). *Strengthening school counseling and college advising: San Diego State University White House Post Convening Report.* San Diego, CA: http://www.cescal.org/documents/White%20House%20Post%20Convening%20Report.p

Herr, E. L. (2001). The impact of national policies, economics, and school reform on comprehensive guidance programs. *Professional School Counseling*, *4*(4), 236.

House, R. M., & Hayes, R. L. (2002). School counselors: Becoming key players in school reform. *Professional School Counseling*, *5*, 249–256.

Ladson-Billings, G. (2000). Fighting for our lives. *Journal of Teacher Education*, *51*(3), 206–214. 10.1177/0022487100051003008

Lareau, A., & Horvat, E. M. (1999). Moments of social inclusion and exclusion race, class, and cultural capital in family-school relationships. *Sociology of Education*, *72*(1), 37–53. 10.2307/2673185

National Office for School Counselor Advocacy (2011). *2011 National survey of school counselors: Counseling at a crossroads.* Washington, DC: College Board Advocacy & Policy Center. [NOSCA]

No Child Left Behind Act of 2001, P.L. 107-110, 20 U.S.C. § 6319 (2002).

O'Neil, J. M., & Denke, R. (2016). An empirical review of gender role conflict research: New conceptual models and research paradigms.

Perusse, R., Goodnough, G. E., Donegan, J., & Jones, C. (2004). Perceptions of school counselors and school principals about the national standards for school counseling programs and the transforming school counseling initiative. *Professional School Counseling*, 152–161.

Chapter 6

College and Career Counseling, Aspirations, and Achievement

Key Terms (See Chapter 1)
Minority Serving Institutions (MSI), Historically Black Colleges and Universities (HBCUs), Hispanic-Serving Institutions (HSIs), Tribal Colleges and Universities (TCUs)

Author Narrative: Amber Sansbury

I reflect and discuss the impact of access, school resources, and opportunities afforded a magnet setting situated in a predominantly White neighborhood. The experience of opportunity was apparent but did it come at a cost of attending a high school that perpetuated the dominant culture's competitive nature, the absence of a collectivist framework, and the impact of microaggressions? I attended a Columbus, Georgia, magnet high school from 2000 to 2004. It was annually rated the No. 1 school in the state and had wonderful counselors that presented open doors as I prepared for college. My narrative and the related positive school structures exemplify the findings in Witty and Jenkins's (1935) "The Case of 'B' – A Gifted Negro Girl."

My sisters and I grew up in an African American family living in a predominantly White middle-class neighborhood in Columbus, Georgia. Our married parents worked hard to maintain economic stability, preserved Christian traditions, and engaged with our learning often. I am not a first-generation college student or doctoral student. I have the privilege of having immediate and extended family members who have earned doctoral degrees and guided me along the way. Leading up to high school graduation, my school counselors reached out to me often to inquire about my goals and direction. They provided valuable resources about applying for college at Emory University, the University of Georgia, and several other great schools to which I was accepted. I ultimately decided on a smaller state school where I obtained a full scholarship, annual stipend,

DOI: 10.4324/9781003226253-8

and college support through Air Force ROTC. I am thankful for the level of support and options that were afforded at a magnet high school with many resources.

Keenly, I am aware that today's Black students may not access the same opportunities leading up to college and career transition. School counselors may have set notions on what next steps are appropriate or reasonable instead of the "skies the limit" philosophy that shaped my experience due to high expectations of and for me. Unlike my own, Black parents may work in low-wage industries or irregular hours, which impacts their ability to extend enrichment or come to school activities. This reality affects how too many families are perceived and perform acceptable parenting behaviors in schools. Precious resources for students are often awarded through learning the system of rewards vis-à-vis navigational capital. This chapter challenges us all to upend assumptions about at what stages, when, and *how* college and career counseling occurs through school counseling – especially for groups of historically excluded students.

Content

There is a shortage of research on the creation and exploration of college-going culture at the elementary, middle, and high school levels. The authors will describe the value of community partnerships and the role of key stakeholders. Moreover, the authors encourage the reader to consider the role of a school counselor as students prepare for college and careers at the primary and secondary levels. In this chapter, we will look at how school counselors can take a more inclusive approach to college and career planning to provide representation for students as well as a sense of pride and confirmation of opportunity for those they serve. What are some areas school counselors can better engage in (partnerships with students and their families, IHEs, disability services, community-based nonprofits, etc.) to expand possibilities? As school counselors, we are charged with the task of promoting the academic, social, emotional, and career needs of our students. The authors will explore college and career readiness at both the primary and secondary levels. In addition, a case study is used to illustrate the college and career trajectory of a biracial male as he transitions from K–12 to postsecondary success. Within this chapter, the authors will outline the decisions made in supporting this student and the infused theoretical approaches supporting the college and career development of racial/ethnic minoritized children. Table 6.1.

Table 6.1 Holland's Theory of Career Choice. Image created by Author, Shekila Melchior

Growth Stage	Children are in a skill development phase developing ideas about work and career.
Exploratory Stage	Occupational awareness, fantasy play, awareness of choices followed by choice is made.
Establishment Stage	The individual enters the job market, "tries it on for size" and then possibly makes the transition to find their "fit".
Maintenance Stage	Develop skills for success and satisfaction.
Disengagement Stage	During this stage, the individual's focus has diminished and they're ready for retirement.

Theories of Career Development

Holland (1959)

Holland's Theory of Career Choice (See Table 6.1) suggests that individuals choose their careers based on their personality and environment. The Theory of Career Choice (RIASEC) maintains that individuals choose careers and/or jobs in which they can be around individuals similar to themselves. Moreover, individuals will seek out environments that will allow them to utilize their abilities and express their values and attitudes. In theory, individuals who choose a job that fits their type (RIASEC) will work in a more enjoyable environment (Figure 6.1).

Super (1953)

Super's Career Development Theory enlists a developmental perspective for understanding careers. Super enlists a life span approach that expands Career exploration beyond the traditional understanding of career exploration during the young adult stage. Drawing upon the work of developmental psychologists, Super outlines five stages for career development, with each characterized by three to four development tasks. The five stages conceptualize the impact of childhood ideas and play on career choice and work satisfaction.

Krumboltz et al. (1976)

Krumboltz's Social Learning Theory posits that learning is an important aspect of the ever-changing workplace, impacting the behavioral, emotional, and cognitive aspects of the individual. Krumboltz believes that career development happens through learning concepts, work habits, role modeling, and attitudes. When considering college and career readiness in

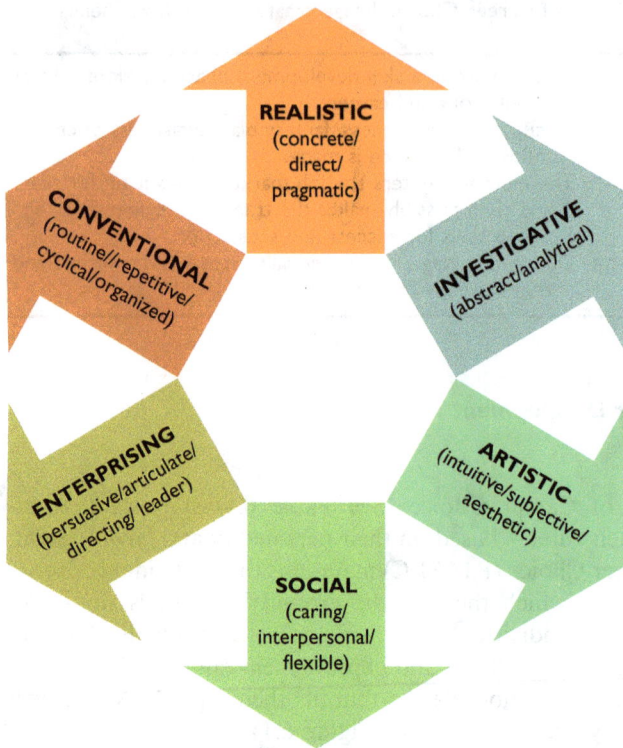

Figure 6.1 Holland's Theory of Career Choice. Image created by Author, Shekila Melchior.

a primary and secondary setting, one can identify some overlapping concepts in this theory. Krumboltz offers that utilizing a task approach builds new behaviors and role models can have a positive or negative impact on the individual's career development.

Gottfredson (1981)

Gottfredson's theory of Circumscription and Compromise centers on the notion that how one is situated in society based on the identities they hold can ultimately influence their career choice. Gottfredson theorizes that a child's awareness develops unconsciously around what is deemed an acceptable career for the identities they hold. For example, if a young Black woman rarely sees Black physicians while growing up, then she may adjust her career choice based on the lack of representation. Gottfredson

Table 6.2 Gottfredson's theory of Circumscription and Compromise

Orientation to Size and Power (Age 3–5)	Orientation to Sex Roles (Age 6–8)	Orientation to Social Values (Age 9–13)	Orientation to the Internal, Unique Self (Age 14+)
During this stage, children become aware of the roles adults have, and that eventually they will become an adult and take on the role themselves.	During this stage, children begin to categorize roles by gender. Children in this stage assign job roles to specific genders.	During this stage, children begin to classify job roles within social status as well as gender. They begin to identify some job roles as unacceptable.	During this final stage, adolescents are more conscious of job roles and begin using their interests and abilities to identify job options to include and/or eliminate.

offers that circumscription happens in four stages (see above), followed by compromise. Compromise is described as the stage in which individuals sacrifice roles for what they perceive to be more accessible or more beneficial to their microsystem (Table 6.2).

Activity

Bandura's theory (1977) focuses on self-efficacy, and an individual's capability to achieve their plan is a central tenant. Upon reviewing the theory, reflect on how the tenets could support diverse students' career development or serve as a barrier. Compare Bandura's theory to Lent, Brown & Hackett's (1996) Social Cognitive Career Theory. What similarities and differences do you notice? How might you apply this to your work?

Frameworks/Initiatives

Several frameworks and initiatives have emerged in support of college and career development for school counselors: The National Career Development Guidelines; The Reach Higher Initiatives; the College Board Eight Components; and ASCA's Mindsets and Behaviors and Position Statements.

Reach Higher

Michelle Obama launched the Reach Higher Initiative in 2014 to inspire students to pursue postsecondary opportunities. Her initiative supports efforts such as training programs/apprenticeships and two- and four-year colleges and universities. The overarching goals of the initiative are to:

1 Provide insight into postsecondary opportunities;
2 Inform students of financial aid options for college affordability;
3 Motivate students to participate in academic planning; and
4 Support school counselors' (specifically high school counselors) work in college and career readiness.

National Career Development Guidelines (NCDG)

The National Career Development Guidelines (NCDG) is a framework utilized in several counties across the United States. The NCDG is organized into three domains: Personal Social Development (PS), Educational Achievement and Lifelong Learning (ED), and Career Management (CM). Each domain has a goal. The goals outline broader areas of competency for career development and include indicators of mastery based on the knowledge and skills individuals need to achieve goals. In 2009, NCDA added multicultural competencies to the guidelines to ensure college counseling professionals could demonstrate both knowledge and skills when working with diverse populations. The guidelines are further expounded upon in the primary and secondary level portion of the chapter.

National Office of School Counselor Advocacy

The College Board's major mission has been to provide a gateway to higher education using sophisticated educational testing endeavors that primarily benefited financially stable citizens. However, in 2007, the College Board commissioned the National Office of School Counselor Advocacy (NOSCA), which provided a platform within the College Board to initiate and promote a framework that consisted of eight components of college and career readiness counseling. The research, primarily derived from school counselors' and school administrators' collaborative efforts for improvement, was substantial enough to offer the following eight components for school counselors to use when engaging in college and career readiness. These components are summarized below and also in Hines et al. (2020).

The eight components (College Board) are:

1 College Aspirations

   a Goal: Build a college-going culture based on early college awareness by nurturing in students the confidence to aspire to college and the resilience to overcome challenges along the way. Maintain high expectations by providing adequate support, building social capital, and conveying the conviction that all students can succeed in college.

2   Academic Planning for College and Career Readiness

a   Goal: Advance students' planning, preparation, participation, and performance in a rigorous academic program that connects to their college and career aspirations and goals.

3   Enrichment and Extracurricular Engagement

a   Goal: Ensure equitable exposure to a wide range of extracurricular and enrichment opportunities that build leadership, nurture talents and interests, and increase engagement with school.

4   College and Career Exploration and Selection Processes

a   Goal: Provide early and ongoing exposure to experiences and information necessary to make informed decisions when selecting a college or career that connects to academic preparation and future aspirations.

5   College and Career Assessments

a   Goal: Promote preparation, participation, and performance in college and career assessments by all students.

6   College Affordability Planning

a   Goal: Provide students and families with comprehensive information about college costs, options for paying for college, and the financial aid and scholarship processes and eligibility requirements, so they can plan for and afford a college education.

7   College and Career Admission Processes

a   Goal: Ensure that students and families have an early and ongoing understanding of the college and career application and admission processes so they can find the postsecondary options that are the best fit with their aspirations and interests.

8   Transition from High School Graduation to College Enrollment

a   Goal: Connect students to school and community resources to help the students overcome barriers and ensure a successful transition from high school to college.

ASCA Position Statements on College Career Readiness

Career Development	This position statement outlines the role of the school counselor in student career development.
College Access Profession	This position statement outlines the collaborative relationship between school counselors and college access professionals.
Individual Student Planning	This position statement outlines the proactive role the school counselor takes in academic planning that contributes to postsecondary plans.
Career and Technical Education (CTE)	This position statement outlines the importance of the school counselor's knowledge and support of CTE Programs
Student Post-Secondary Recruitment	This position statement outlines the role of the school counselor as an advocate for all students during their postsecondary recruitment process, aiding students and families in their decision-making.

Equity and Access in College and Career Readiness

Through a lens of social justice and advocacy, school counselors can enlist culturally appropriate interventions. Career interventions based on the specific needs of racially minoritized students are necessary to reduce opportunity gaps and increase career options.

There is one creative study that explores the impact on career-related variables resulting from participation in a culturally responsive career development program (Routledge & Gnikla, 2022). This 15-week after-school program was designed and implemented to foster growth and development in career exploration and leadership as well as career decision-making self-efficacy. The creativity to combat racism while fueling career development and positive racial identity development serves as a great model for other school counselors and researchers. Results provide initial support in suggesting that culturally responsive career development programs impact the career development of minority girls, especially in the areas of student motivation and engagement and perceived career barriers.

Career Development for 21st-Century Scholars

There are three critical considerations to make to teach students skills to enter the workforce:

1 We must include opportunities for learning within and beyond the classroom.

2 The characteristics we deem important and want to teach to our students, we must learn and practice for ourselves. For example, school counselors can model good listening skills. We can allow the students an opportunity to advance our understanding by engaging in listening to their perspectives. To illustrate further, we can learn much from technology and digital modalities from our students. There are no limits to the exchange of ideas. But does all of this work take place only during the school day?

3 In schools, school counselors can create programs that provide room for students and school staff to engage in critical discourse. These strategies to give and collaboratively receive feedback could increase positive outcomes. These interactions must be built upon respect for one another and be flexible enough to maneuver difficulties. In all of these endeavors, remember to be creative and thoughtful, and welcoming, even if only sharing your ideas. Within the classroom ideas can be generated; however, the work can take place within the school or the broader local, national, or global communities. For example, we all understand that health and well-being are more important now than ever before. We also recognize that this is nonnegotiable and that maintaining good health is a form of resistance. Is it possible that some of the ideas generated to make a local impact can be applied to the global community?

Primary and Secondary Settings

Elementary School

School counselors are encouraged to increase awareness of self and begin to understand broad concepts of work during elementary school. They begin viewing career roles through a gendered lens. At this early stage of development, school counselors should diversify career representation and encourage exploration. With strategic partnerships during primary education, school counselors can work with grade-level teachers to build on "Career Day" events, ultimately planting seeds for children to explore their college development throughout their education.

a What information, if any, was shared with you about college and career during your primary school years?

b If you are representative of a diverse population, did you see yourself in the professions you had an interest in?

c Were your dreams nurtured early on? Were you allowed to dream or to operate from a realistic perspective?

Middle School

As students make the transition into middle school, we see a sharp increase in their desire for independence and the influence of peers. Students begin to formulate plans and goals around specific careers and become more insightful about the possibility of the future. Middle school begins to introduce relevant courses and career assessments to aid students in finding careers that fit the overall personality or interests of students. For school counselors in middle schools, partnering with a local college/university to discuss pathways to achieve those careers may offer support to the high school planning that takes place in eighth grade.

a   What career paths were you most interested in during middle school? Did you receive support (i.e., information about clubs, coursework, internships, and role models) around that career path?
b   As a school counselor, what potential biases might arise in college and career choice? How could individual biases impact the support they offer students?
c   From your observations, what professions were most celebrated in middle school? Was it doctors, nurses, and engineers? Were individuals from trade professions highlighted as of equal importance? If not, why might you think that is?

High School

High school is when we see the majority of students begin to solidify their potential college and career path. Students are ideally preparing themselves for their postsecondary opportunities. They may, at this time, become more realistic about what they hope to achieve. Special attention should be given to the anxiety that surrounds the college choice process and the support that can be offered by school counselors. Additionally, the consciousness of barriers that could impact the progress of diverse students is imperative. School counselors should be at the forefront of ensuring all educators in the building are providing students with the best opportunity to achieve their goals. During my (Shekila's) time as a high school counselor, we opted to hold an additional college fair aside from the traditional four-year institution fair. We held a two-year technical trade fair for students who wanted to pursue postsecondary opportunities in trade professions. Additionally, we hosted a tour for students with an interest in attending Historically Black Colleges and Universities (HBCUs).

a   As a school counselor, what innovative ideas have you considered when working with high school students?

b What barriers to college and career choices have you observed in a high school setting?
c Reflect on your own journey towards postsecondary success, did you receive the help you needed? If not, what would have improved your experience?

Activity: A Case Study (where the relevant ASCA Mindsets and Behaviors for Student Success [2021] are cited)

Let's introduce the case study for this chapter. In the future, Qahlil is an upper-middle-class biracial male living by choice with a single father, who identifies as Black. He holds a graduate-level education and has previous experience with the higher education system.

As a child, Qahlil entered kindergarten with some concerns about ADHD presented by his pre-K teacher; psychological assessments were conducted in his first year. His school counselor recommended gifted testing as well. The rationale behind the gifted testing was to rule out the potential that Qahlil was simply bored in the classroom. Qahlil indicated that his long-term goal is to be a doctor and a firefighter. Despite some inattentiveness in the classroom, he was academically strong.

Qahlil: Kindergartento Grade 5 of Elementary School

As noted in the introduction, Qahlil's family was encouraged to have a psychological assessment conducted for ADHD, and he tested as gifted. After the assessments Qahlil was diagnosed with ADHD as well as being gifted; he was given a 504 plan and resources to assist with his executive functioning skills. The issues that were presented to the school counselor were inattentiveness and difficulty with time management. Most notably, his inattentiveness was apparent in kindergarten through second grade, but seemed to improve with the change of teacher from third grade to fifth grade. The school counselor's observation of the lack of connection between the teacher and Qahlil allowed her to bridge the gap to ensure that he continued to excel academically.

- **ASCA Mindsets**

  - Belief in the development of the whole self, including a healthy balance of mental, social/emotional, and physical well-being.
  - Self-confidence in the ability to succeed.
  - Belief in using abilities to their fullest to achieve high-quality results and outcomes.

- **Reimagined**

  - School counselors are encouraged to reflect on any potential bias that inhibits student progress and a sense of belonging in a classroom. Additionally, care should be given to neurodivergent students and nurturing their self-confidence.

- **Questions**

  - When considering the intersecting identities of Qahlil, what should the counselor consider when offering him support?
  - What possible biases may skew the school counselor's lens when supporting him?
  - Are there any career theories that you may find helpful at this stage of his development?

Qahlil: Sixth through Eighth Grade of Middle School

Arriving in middle school, Qahlil continued to struggle with inattentiveness, which ultimately led to behavioral concerns. The school counselor from his elementary school held a conference meeting with Qahlil's father and the new school counselor to better understand how to support him. Qahlil was placed in several honors-level courses and accelerated math courses during middle school. At this time, he began to excel in sports, which helped support his time management and attentiveness in the classroom. During his career exploration, he began to show a vested interest in engineering, working on vehicles, and building robots. The school counselor recommended that Qahlil join the school's robotics team and enroll in the industrial and mechanical classes that were held at both the middle school and the high school. It was during this time that Qahlil's love of engineering grew. During a career assessment test given in the eighth grade, Qahlil scored high in engineering and mathematics. His support system at home placed him in summer camp each year to help nurture his budding interest, along with his extracurricular activities in sports.

- **ASCA Mindsets**

  - Belief in the development of the whole self, including a healthy balance of mental, social/emotional, and physical well-being.
  - M 4. Self-confidence in the ability to succeed.
  - Belief in using abilities to their fullest to achieve high-quality results and outcomes.

- **Reimagined**

  - Nurturing student dreams, creating pathways representation of those currently in the profession. Addressing the child with honest and clear communication will allow them to identify techniques and areas of strength that will assist them in any potential challenges.

- **Questions**

  - When considering the intersecting identities of Qahlil, what should the counselor consider when offering him support?
  - What possible biases may skew the school counselor's lens when supporting him?
  - Are there any career theories that you may find helpful at this stage of his development?

Qahlil: Ninth through Twelfth Grade of High School

Qahlil has now transitioned into the last four years of his K–12 academic career. He is excelling in both soccer and baseball and has joined several clubs to further strengthen his resume. Qahlil no longer struggles with behavioral issues; however, his performance has led to some experiences of anxiety and over-performing in the classroom. The school counselor has met with Qahlil to offer him various techniques to manage his anxiety and to identify extracurricular activities that he might let go of. Overcommitted, Qahlil is currently enrolled in all honors classes in ninth and tenth grade, and one AP class in tenth grade. In eleventh grade, he decided to enroll in three AP classes with the intention of enrolling in five AP classes his senior year. He has a goal of attending an Ivy League institution and obtaining a high score on his SAT. Qahlil continues to maintain a 4.0 GPA and excels in his extracurricular activities. He does however, notice that his anxiety continues to increase the more he takes on academically and with extracurriculars; the school counselor meets with both him and his father to explore what would allow Qahlil to continue to be successful while also maintaining his mental health. Qahlil opts to take only two AP classes in his senior year. He will continue to play soccer and baseball and will only participate in the Black student organization and National Honor Society. Outside of school, he will limit his community service to the church while also participating in a robotics team.

- **ASCA Mindsets**

  - Sense of acceptance, respect, support, and inclusion for self and others in the school environment

- Belief in using abilities to their fullest to achieve high-quality results and outcomes.
- Understanding that postsecondary education and lifelong learning are necessary for long-term success.

- **Reimagined**

    - High-achieving students' identities can be grounded in their accomplishments, leading to a disconnect between caring for their mental health and achieving goals to move them forward post-high school. Encourage adolescents to pursue their goals and strive for success through a holistic lens, to identify what success looks like both professionally and personally. Perhaps, students can better accept and respect themselves if they realize they are more than grades, scores, and college acceptances.

- **Questions**

    - When considering the intersecting identities of Qahlil, what should the counselor consider when offering him support?
    - What possible biases may skew the school counselor's lens when supporting him?
    - Are there any career theories that you may find helpful at this stage of his development?

Postsecondary Education

Of the offers received, Qahlil decides to pursue Mechanical Engineering at North Carolina A&T State University with a full scholarship. As discussed in previous chapters, the fostering of racial socialization contributed to Qahlil's decision to attend an HBCU. Qahlil remains hesitant, wondering if he should have pursued his athletic dreams in college. Ultimately, he decides that the path of engineering is a better fit. During his collegiate experience, he joins a fraternity, participates in service activities, and acquires an internship at one of the top engineering firms in North Carolina. Upon the completion of his degree, he accepts an entry-level engineering position in Chicago, Illinois. He later goes on to become a lead engineer in his field.

Summary

Career development and professional identity remain critical areas that need addressing for young Black and Brown children. Career interventions based on the specific needs of racially minoritized students are necessary to reduce opportunity gaps and increase career options (Routledge, 2022).

Currently, racial-ethnic minorities continue to face disparities educationally and economically. Black and Brown girls often are subjected to "double jeopardy" as they navigate a world still ridden with racial and gender discrimination. These barriers and other social and environmental factors have negatively impacted career self-efficacy, resulting in a lack of appropriate career decision-making. Through a lens of social justice and advocacy, school counselors can act as allies and provide culturally appropriate interventions that address these disparate outcomes and processes, unlocking all students' potential for success and well-being into adulthood.

Key Takeaways

1 Many factors can influence College Career Choice (CCC) (e.g., a school counselor's beliefs, school norms, and existing relationships with students).
2 It is necessary to reflect on your personal experiences that impact the CCC.
3 Developing partnerships that promote positive CCC is needed in schools.
4 A student-centered approach to college and career readiness that is developmentally appropriate and culturally responsive needs to be created.

Application

1 Consider your own experiences. What differences would you have liked to see when you were engaging in the college choice process?
2 How have you engaged in your work as a result of your own experiences?
3 As a school counselor, how might you explore any potential implicit biases you hold against racially minoritized students and their ability to succeed in their postsecondary planning?
4 What are the things that are missing and what are the parts of the conversations that haven't been addressed?
5 How has technology changed the world of work, college, and career?
6 How have recent shifts in the social-political culture created opportunities or further exacerbated disparities?

References

American School Counselor Association (2021). *The school counselor and individual student planning for postsecondary preparation*. Alexandria, VA: Author.

American School Counselor Association (2021). *The school counselor and career development*. Alexandria, VA: Author.

American School Counselor Association (2021). *The school counselor and student post secondary recruitment*. Alexandria, VA: Author.

American School Counselor Association (2018). *The school counselor and career and technical education*. Alexandria, VA: Author.

American School Counselor Association (2021). *ASCA student standards; mindsets and behaviors for student success*. Alexandria, VA: Author.

American School Counselor Association (2021). *The school counselor and college access professionals*. Alexandria, VA: Author.

Bandura, A. (1977). *Social learning theory*. Prentice-Hall.

College Board. (2010). *College Board*. Eight Components of College and Career Readiness Counseling. Retrieved February 1, 2023, from https://secure-media. collegeboard.org/digitalServices/pdf/nosca/11b_4416_8_Components_WEB_111107.pdf

Gottfredson, L. S. (1981). Circumscription and compromise: A developmental theory of occupational aspirations [Monograph]. *Journal of Counseling Psychology, 28*, 545–579.

Holland, J. L. (1959). A theory of vocational choice. *Journal of Counseling Psychology, 6*, 35–45.

Hines, E. M., Hines, M. R., Moore III, J. L., Steen, S., Singleton, P., Cintron, D., ... & Henderson, J. (2020). Preparing African American males for college: A group counseling approach. *The Journal for Specialists in Group Work, 45*(2), 129–145.

Jenkins, M. D. (1939). The mental ability of the American Negro. *The Journal of Negro Education, 8*(3), 511–520. 10.2307/2292647

Krumboltz, J. D., Mitchell, A. M., & Jones, G. B. (1976). A social learning theory of career selection. *The Counseling Psychologist, 6*(1), 71–81.

Lent, R. W., Brown, S. D., & Hackett, G. (1994). Toward a unifying social cognitive theory of career and academic interest, choice, and performance. *Journal of Vocational Behavior, 45*, 79–122.

National Career Development Association. (2004). *National career development guidelines framework*. Author. https://www.ncda.org/aws/NCDA/asset_manager/get_file/3384?ver=7802067

Reach Higher Initiative (2015). Retrieved from https://www.whitehouse.gov/reach-higher

Rutledge, Marsha L. & Gnilka, Philip B. (2022) Breaking Down Barriers: A Culturally Responsive Career Development Intervention with Racially Minoritized Girls of Color. *Journal of College Access, 7*(1), Article 7. Available at: https://scholarworks.wmich.edu/jca/vol7/iss1/7

Rutledge, M. (2022). From Traditional to Tailored: How School Counselors Should Consider the Career Development Needs of Minoritized Youth.

Super, D. E. (1953). A theory of vocational development. *American Psychologist, 8*(5), 185–190.

Chapter 7

School Counselor Identity, Consultation, Collaboration, and Supervision

Key Terms (See Chapter 1)
Consultation, School Counseling Supervision Parent Liasiason and Family Engagement

Author Narrative: Sam Steen

My professional school counselor identity can be traced back to one person during my graduate school program. My academic adviser was an assistant professor who had recently left work as a full-time school counselor to pursue a PhD, and she worked in the master's program I was attending. She was the first and only Black/African American professor I had spanning my higher education experience. She was a role model for success who had a strong work ethic. She encouraged my success in the master's program despite the educational barriers I faced during my undergraduate program. I had no idea of the number of professional opportunities that would emerge for me once I would earn my master's degree in counseling. She made me believe that I could accomplish anything and, along the way, she challenged her students to strive for perfection. She modeled classroom teaching lessons, professional dispositions, and a balance between school-based practice and research. She was actively publishing, giving presentations, and commuting from Virginia to New Jersey, where she and her husband resided. These early professional experiences, preparation, and modeling shaped my school counseling identity, allowing me to confidently enter schools knowing that I could help all students, not just Black and Brown students. Dr. Norma Day-Vines, the professor who is now a good friend, treated all of her students with warmth while maintaining high expectations. From these early experiences, we aim to reaffirm the influence that a committed school counselor can make on the lives of all students with whom they come in contact.

DOI: 10.4324/9781003226253-9

Content

It is important to note that relationship building can allow school personnel to gain clarity for a better understanding of the "c" culture of families. Oftentimes, there is mistrust resulting from cultural mismatches and assumptions/biases made based on the lens through which you view family (Posey-Maddox, 2017).

In other words, implicit biases can influence your relationships with parents and families, beliefs about home environments, and interpretations of families' decisions (Young & Bryan, 2018). School counselors must view families as assets and not deficits. It is critical for school personnel to believe that parents and children should remain together. Parent fitness should be reviewed and not necessarily questioned, and families should be granted the belief that they want the best education for their children.

Advocacy for the School Counseling Profession

School counselors are often misrepresented, leading to a lack of awareness of their roles and responsibilities. School counselors may not be able to create their dream school counseling program due to limited resources or a lack of support from a specific school setting. Ultimately, a school counselor is an advocate for their students. We seek to provide academic, career, and college guidance, as well as to foster a safe, welcoming environment where students grow in their social-emotional competencies and mental health. Counselors must be culturally aware and knowledgeable of the sensitivities of the current social systems that impact students, whether they are in school or out of it. The school counselor also must have strong communication skills to collaborate with administration, teachers, students, families, and community partners who may be supporting students directly or indirectly.

Rationale for School Counseling Program

The highlighted differentiation between mundane school counselors and recognized school counselors is those who strive to close the achievement gap. The Recognized ASCA (American School Counselor Association) Model Program (RAMP) is used to determine if the decisions, implementation, and application of student data, deliver school programs that are efficient and effective for all students. The purpose is to ensure that, systematically, a developmentally appropriate curriculum is focused on the mindsets and behaviors of all students, preparing them to succeed, and improving overall student achievement, attendance, and discipline. These are lofty goals and are lacking in inclusive language that moves beyond the generic. Consider the following prompts about the RAMP program:

- What are the pros of such a program?
- What are the cons of such a program?
- After a school is RAMPed, should it have to reRAMP?
- How long do you think it should be before a school should reRAMP?
- How much time do you think it takes to RAMP?
- To what extent could the time and resources used to demonstrate to outside officials that the school counseling program is effective be used to support students?

These school counselors shine in their department and do so by aligning their school counseling program to the school's academic mission (ASCA, 2019), providing services to students in determining their progress towards this mission. One strategy ASCA uses to bring consistency to the profession across the U.S. is its RAMP awards. RAMP awards measure whether the institution-to-institution school counseling program aligns with the ASCA National Model. RAMP recognition benefits school counselors in their program evaluation by identifying areas in need of improvement, truncating to three program goals, and specific target gap issues (Johnson et.al., 2010). However, school counselors are hesitant from executing decisions regarding student performance, despite conclusive data, due to several factors. These factors include conflict with school professionals, which can happen when confronting educational barriers. School staff overburdened with administrative tasks may be unable or unwilling to use the data that is available to make decisions (Holcomb-McCoy et al., 2009).

Evidence indicates that employing school counseling accountability strategies as an outcome of collecting and analyzing data can lead to improved student performance and productivity and, ultimately, program effectiveness (Young & Kaffenberger, 2011). Leaders in policy-making and counseling recognize the influence of data to apprise academic and instructional results; the No Child Left Behind Act (NCLB) of 2001 necessitates that each state implement a statewide accountability arrangement addressing the academic needs of all students (U.S. Department of Education, 2010). Many central office administrators utilize data to manipulate decisions that amend instruction, demonstrate progress toward meeting state standards, justify program funding and personnel, and determine professional development needs (Whiston, 1996). Most recently, A Blueprint for Reform: The Reauthorization of Elementary and Secondary Education Act (U.S. Department of Education, 2010) detected targeted education reform efforts to take on previous reforms such as NCLB and the American Recovery and Reinvestment Act of 2009 (Zandi, 2009). School participants, faculty, and administration are expected to collect, analyze and elucidate data to understand the necessary steps to close the achievement gap. School counselors can use data within their school counseling programs to create equity and access for all students.

Researchers reported that when school counselors' self-efficacy had a stronger correlation with a data-usage inclination with higher school counselor self-efficacy, there was a lucid methodology to identify achievement gaps in their buildings and subsequently use the ASCA Model as an outline for their school counseling programs (Holcomb- McCoy et al., 2009). For school counselors to improve self-efficacy and inclination for data usage, there are four factors to be addressed that can not only improve the individual counselors, but also the institutions as a whole. First, the implementation of comprehensive programs based on the respective goals, aligned with data, is to be applied across all domains (ASCA, 2019). Second, school counselors are to abide by data to ensure access to organic services and resources for all students and maintain this standard. Third, school counselors are challenged when multitasking between academic advising, career counseling, and higher learning enrollment (McDonough, 2005). It is important to note that early higher education opportunities encourage students to seek information and any further actions necessary for academic and self-growth. A wide spectrum of students fills the classroom seats, and among those are students from minoritized socioeconomic backgrounds; these students from lower socioeconomic statuses have often received messages to accept a destiny lacking in education. This lack of academic morale indefinitely impacts the achievement gap; therefore, closing the gap via an intensive curriculum and liberal academic access to learning goals will satisfy the academic needs of all students, ensuring no student gets left behind, despite their status (Brown & Trusty, 2005). Fourth, verbal, written, or visual representations of the data should be shared among stakeholders to ensure communication of the findings highlighting school performance, progression, student success, and areas of improvement (Young & Kaffenberger, 2011).

The school counselor plays an instrumental role in ensuring that the data collected is used in the manner in which it is intended. Idealistically, even with proper planning and execution of the aforementioned steps, counselors must embody their own professional integrity (Gysbers & Henderson, 2014). Counselors who can distinguish from their identity and transition from an administrative role confined to a school to an agent in a systemic community will further promote growth and maturity in all students using the available resources (Gysbers & Henderson, 2014). The opportunities supplied by the immediate community advocate for a healthier learning environment; both external and internal assets can make or break the learning system, whether it be the immediate environment or students' interpersonal attitudes. School counselors are leaders and can be role models for school personnel and students. The environment that school counselors are a part of benefits greatly when school counselors function as culturally responsive professionals and social justice advocates. We expand on this concept of school counselor leadership in detail below.

Leadership

When school counselors, teachers, and parents work together to address gaps in achievement, the chances of success improve. More specifically, when school counselors take a leadership role that facilitates liaisons between faculty and family; certain partnership interventions contribute to student achievements (Bryan & Henry, 2008). Publications detail the significance of school counselor-centered interventions in faculty-family environments and essentialize partnerships as a pragmatic approach to accomplishing goals and further narrowing the gap between student success and student failure (Holcomb-McCoy & Bryan, 2010). The core obstacle in accomplishing this feat is not a singular issue, but rather a multifaceted complexity comprised of the social climate of the select institution, academic expectations, and its tracking, school counselor self-efficacy on partnerships, role perceptions, time constraints, and partnership-related training (Holcomb-McCoy & Bryan, 2010). The approach to addressing these concerns requires active participation by all school participants. School counselors can lead a partnership-process model to enable collaboration and mitigate barriers that hinder their partnership involvement.

An ideal model, facilitated by school counselors, would be that which would establish the blueprints to a systematic approach that incorporates efforts from the school, family, and community. Via democratic collaboration, a holistic relationship involving the school, the student, the student's family, and the student's community helps in shared decision-making, ownership, and accountability. The emphasis on this directive is the empowerment of voices that would otherwise be suppressed over a larger authority; the school-family-community model would allow a productive, vocal symphony of contributions. Alongside a vocal openness, this model can also act as a form of "checks-and-balances" that supports wider participation. This allows a perpetual state of supervising and supervision among staff, students, parents, and school counselors, which leads to more effective parent and school relationships (Holcomb-McCoy & Bryan, 2010).

The desegregated nature of this model allows the involvement of voices from dissimilar socioeconomic statuses without the social stigma labeled to each status – the absence of the stigma allows for various backgrounds to stage upon unequivocal grounds and establish both diagnoses and prognoses to enable family and community empowerment and social justice. The former focuses on ameliorating articulations on behalf of family and students' academic success, whereas the latter centralizes access to resources, information, skills, and knowledge for families (Bryan & Henry, 2012). The school-family-community model juxtaposes counselors and other school staff with traditionally racial/ethnic minoritized populations, students, and families to develop relevant agendas allowing families access to progressive classes, healthcare, and academic and higher learning programs. Racial/ethnic minoritized populations are ensured participation in school board and community decision-making, allowing underrepresented families to mitigate barriers to their child's success (Bryan & Henry, 2012).

Partnerships that employ social justice traits reinforce social capital for families, such as facilitating professional networking and elevating social norms that would otherwise be risky for racial/ethnic minoritized populations families. Programs and interventions created for the community and by the community ensure increased information and resources, as well as greater networking between students and families. SCs demonstrate leadership when cultivating strengths-focused partnerships by identifying, utilizing, and bolstering integrities and resiliencies in children, families, and communities regarding academic achievement and community participation (Bryan et al., 2019).

We know that school counselors must consider and eliminate their own biases and stereotypes about students and their families, and that doing so positions them to be social capital to minoritized students and families (Bryan et al., 2011). We also know that explicit and implicit biases affect us all and increase the chances of developing inaccurate judgments about children and families who are unique to themselves. One way to mitigate this dilemma is to create culturally sustaining partnerships.

Collaborative Partnerships: Steps to Success

Cultural reciprocity is a reciprocal process in which professionals assess their personal cultural assumptions fundamental to their practice (Bryan et al., 2019). Cultural reciprocity will ensure better counselor-family relationships to mitigate progress toward students' personal and academic goals. A vision for partnerships is vital and is part of a three-step procedure to relate to the aforementioned seven-part cycle of the school-family-community model. It is critical at this initial step to align planning on behalf of the counselor, family, and academic administration to influence certain, counselor-specific expectations (Bryan & Griffin, 2010). The next step is data-driven, in which school counselors should be inclined to use the data on student outcomes and the needs of various student groups to exhibit a basis for partnership interventions (Bryan & Henry, 2012). Finally, school counselors should lead the vacant opportunities of faculty-and-administration meetings and counselor-led faculty development workshops to exemplify the vision and benefits of partnerships at other schools as well as in their own schools (Bryan & Griffin, 2010).

School Counseling Supervision

Supervision in school counseling is a multimodal process where the counselor serves as the point of contact for the school and the faculty serves as the point of contact for the university. The SC is the liaison between the school and the university. This model is typical and entails the practice of developing a comprehensive school counseling program, the conceptualization of interventions for students and families, and personalization and the development of strong relationships. Within supervision sessions, observable behavior, clinical skills, and interpersonal skills demonstrated by the school counselor trainees is the focus. The counselor receives feedback on interactions and decisions that are made to ensure they are not based on bias or personal issues with the student.

School Counselor and Teacher Consultation

As a counselor, the task of serving as a mental health professional helps advocate for the needs of the students or for uncovering reasons for behaviors observed in the classroom setting. Children with a mental illness may struggle to find the words to ask for help or may not recognize that they need help which may cause frustration, leading to disruption. School counselors are positioned well to be consultants. SCs work closely with such situations and may start to recognize the patterns that need to be addressed immediately. Students may not always feel comfortable explaining their situation to a teacher or a parent; however, the counselor is always available before, after, and during school hours. In other cases, teachers may not feel comfortable discussing sensitive issues with parents/guardians. Counselors can advocate on behalf of the student by providing background information such as problems the student may be dealing with at home that could be influencing that student's performance. This conversation with the teacher may lead to a better understanding of an open approach to talking to the student. According to a study that examined discipline in the classroom, exclusionary discipline strategies and positive behavior strategies were used on students to analyze the outcome. Researchers found that students showed less negative behavior which required discipline from the teacher in the classroom when a positive and encouraging classroom environment was created. In other words, the positive behavior strategy did show a positive student-teacher relationship, improved scores, and better discipline in the classroom. This essentially meant that students recognized the fairness the teacher demonstrated intentionally (Mitchell & Bradshaw, 2013). For Black students in particular, it is important that they recognize school staff (e.g., teachers, school counselors, and administrators) as having their best interest in mind since staff plays a major influence on course major course or elective selections based on the perceived students' strengths and goals. The counselors see the student holistically from all aspects of their life, whereas a teacher may observe the student's behavior and performance only in a specific discipline, at a specific time of the day, and then develop an opinion about the student based on that observation.

Parental Involvement in Their Child's Educational and Learning Processes

One of the most significant aspects of improved learning outcomes and academic success is linking schools and parents/guardians so that teachers, students, and parents partake in the learning process to enhance its effectiveness. Teaming up with Black families to foster parent-student-teacher collaboration is one fundamental aspect of raising active, engaged, culturally aware, and kind learners across the racial spectrum who contribute constructively to an inclusive society (Posey-Maddox, 2017). See Figure 7.1 to illustrate the relationship between the student and the various stakeholders. The student is centered in this figure. The impact of

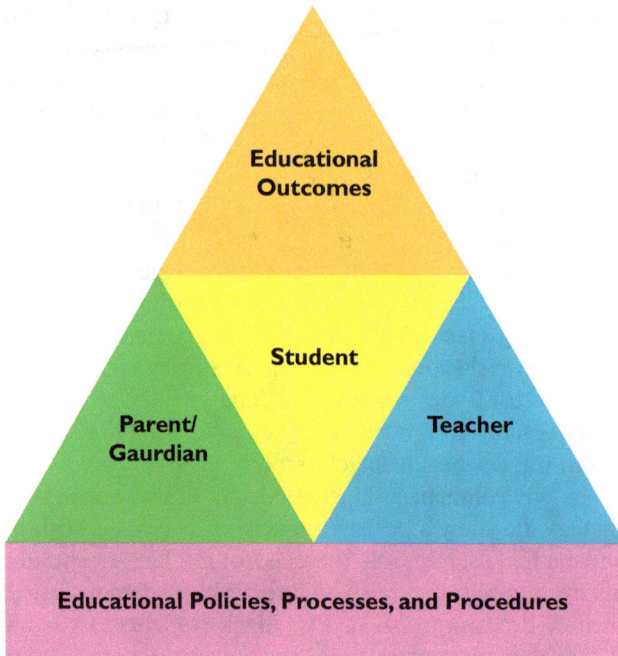

Figure 7.1 Student-Centered Family Engagement.

parents/guardians and teachers is built upon the educational policies, practices, and procedures in the learning process.

Parents/guardians have a vital role in their child's learning process by participating in educational programs, schools, and opportunities throughout their child's educational career. Since parents are the most important stakeholders, they need to know how their involvement can affect their child's future. Teachers and counselors should make it a priority to keep caretakers in the loop in all ongoing activities in the school and to use the family's feedback to devise strategies for further improvement and better execution of educational processes. Parents' feedback – and the parenting goals, contributions, and perspectives that motivate their feedback – helps the SCs and school administrators devise strategies for moving forward.

This meaningful collaboration is a two-way street. The parents who are involved in the academic activities of their child gain knowledge about their child's needs, strengths, weaknesses, and areas for improvement. They tend to support their children in a better way by updating themselves with modern and advanced learning methodologies. The students and teachers benefit from the caretakers' expertise.

The world continues to face the challenges of Covid-19. "Online Education" or "E-Learning" is the new 'normal'. In this mode of distance education, the support and cooperation of parents played a significant role in making learners comfortable with home-based education. Parents/guardians not only helped in using old-fashioned pen and paper, but they also gained experience using a variety of technological modalities and advancements. Families can ensure a better learning environment by continuously upgrading their knowledge of educational technology and digitalization. School counselors working closely with parents/guardians and families can ensure that a deeper understanding of children supports their skill development.

Reinforcement and Communication between Home and School

Parents/guardians know their children well. Through various activities in the early years, parents tend to learn about the fields of interest of their child. School counselors and teachers can collaborate with parents/guardians to help their children explore their fields of interest and to develop an understanding of emerging educational trends and practices that sometimes are hidden from families, especially those who are racial/ethnic minoritized populations. For this, parents could be involved in the educational processes as per the following strategy:

According to the model in Figure 7.2, parents could be involved in learning activities in order to communicate with the teachers in a better way and provide satisfaction to both parties. Through reciprocal relationships, parents should be invited to lead and partner in academic activities in all possible modes of communication. As noted in Figure 7.1 above, there could be a systematic way to engage parents/guardians using the following as guides:

- An equity-focused parent council
- Parent-Teacher, Parent-Counselor, Parent-Teacher-Counselor, Parent-Teacher-Counselor-Student Meetings periodically
- Social networking websites and pages across social media platforms
- Accessible culturally responsive communication emails, mail, brochures, messages, and phone calls
- WhatsApp and media groups
- A culturally inclusive revolving door policy

School Management and counselors should have culturally inclusive revolving-door policies and meetings over prior appointments for the smooth running of the system. Besides academic activities, parents should be invited to other gatherings such as open days, parent breakfast gatherings, parents' sports gala, parents' one-dish parties, parents' talent hunts, etc. Such gatherings will accustom parents to the

Figure 7.2 Parental Involvement in Learning Activities.

school's environment, and parents will consider themselves a "part" of the school's system.

Similarly, parents/guardians belonging to various professions could be invited to conduct career-development seminars for students K–12, with an emphasis on exploration for students from underrepresented backgrounds beginning at an early age. For instance, parents may be invited to share their expertise and various pathways into professions that have historically excluded Black students due to inequitable school resources, course tracking, or biased expectations for college and career readiness. Examples of sustaining, high-demand fields that have been out of reach are:

- Engineering
- Medicine
- Diversity, Equity, and Inclusion (DEI)
- Entrepreneur and Small Business Owner
- Social work
- Psychiatry
- Motivational trainers
- Chefs or Culinary experts
- Fashion design
- Event planning
- Technology and related fields (e.g., software design)
- Marketing
- STEAM robotics
- Accounting
- Health and food safety department
- Law, Judiciary
- E-commerce
- Mental health
- Higher Education, Research, and Academia
- Athletes and Sports Occupations

Continuous engagement of parents/guardians at all stages of learning is key for the holistic development of students and a better understanding of parental roles.

School Counselors Developing and Implementing Parent/Family Training Academy

Recognizing this significant role of parents/caretakers and to better inform and connect them with schooling, educational institutes could create "Parent Academies" to train them in parenting and nurturing the needs of their children, by arranging professional training, workshops, and seminars by experts. This initiative will bridge the gaps in the learning process of the children at school and at home by bringing the necessary stakeholders closer and in continuous and concrete engagement. It will broaden lines of communication among all stakeholders and will vigorously assist the education process to move forward smoothly and effectively. The following is an example of a Parent/Guardian/Family Academy outline created by Ammal Mahmood.

Parent/Guardian/Family Academy - Navigating US Schools and Communities

Goal: To create an educational program that encompasses the specific needs of parents/guardians/extended family networks within our school

Objectives: There are three key objectives to providing educational excellence for our students. In this program, parents/guardians will learn –

1 Information about the role parents can play in their child's educational success;
2 Collaborative and networking opportunities within their communities; and
3 How they can help themselves and their families prosper within and outside of the school community.

In this program, school counselors will facilitate the development, implementation, and evaluation of a Parent/Guardian Academy.

Free workshops, webinars, and classes will be offered for parents and guardians. When relevant, students and family members will be invited to participate. In addition, parents will have the opportunity to participate virtually or physically.

Generally speaking, parents/guardians will explore a wide range of emerging academic, psychological, and social issues. Challenges and opportunities associated with the schooling of the children will be brought into discussion by expert educationists, psychologists, and motivational speakers to engage and inform them in a manner in which they can easily access the presented topics. Engaging parents/guardians/families in this manner will make this initiative more effective, fruitful, and impact-oriented.

Specific Topics to be considered for the Workshops include: (Figure 7.3).

Parenting in the age of digitalization	Career and post-secondary opportunities	Parent involvement at home	Cultivating multiple intelligences
Tuning into your child's unique strengths	Understanding academic and developmental changes for children and adolescent	Building social skills at home and in school	Understanding the social constructs that
Parenting styles	Developing problem solving and stress management skills for the family	Hygiene and healthy eating	Promoting independence at home
Teaching your child how to self-regulate	Family mental health and wellness	Facilitating kindness at home and in school	Using community resources to stimulate learning at home

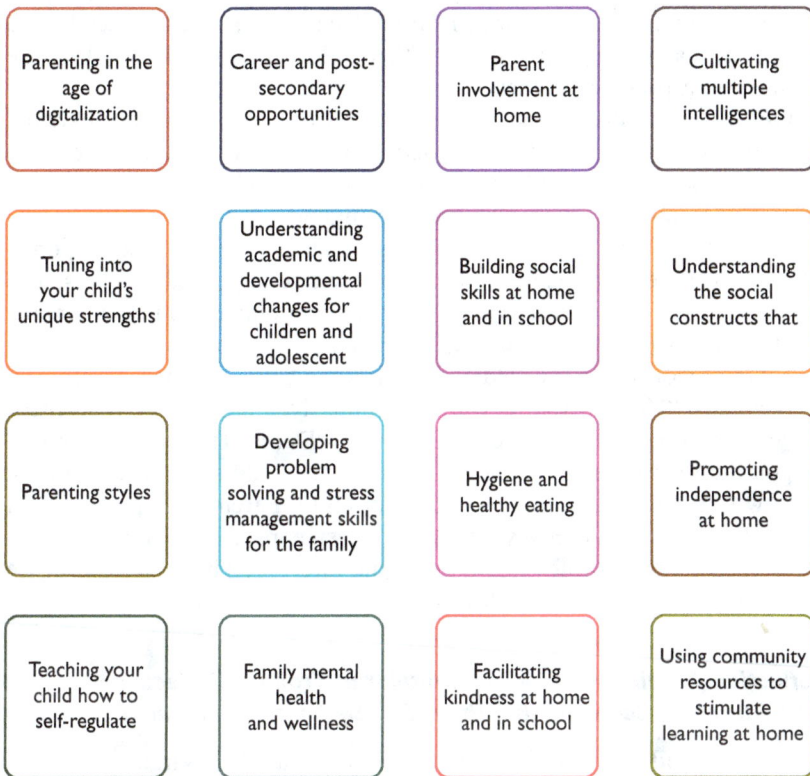

Figure 7.3 Parent Workshop Topics.

Strategies to Engage Parents/Guardians/Families in the Academy

1 Parent and family catalog: A web-based and/or hard copy of a catalog should be designed to inform all parents/guardians well before time about the key ideas, aims, and objectives of the Parent Academy at school. It should include dates of sessions/seminars, topics, a brief introduction about the presenter and session descriptions, and should be shared with all parents/guardians and teachers.

2 School's Event Catalog: Schools can use their own calendar of such seminars with all details and schedules. School personnel should take responsibility for making all necessary arrangements for the parenting sessions. Parents should attend these sessions along with teachers and counselors to learn and explore parenting and nurturing young minds as a team.

3　Invitation Letter to Parents/Family: A formal invitation should be emailed and/or mailed home to parents/guardians at least a week before the seminar to help them balance their other commitments and ensure maximum presence in these sessions.

4　General Announcements: To ensure the strong involvement of parents/guardians/families and their active participation, announcements should be made on all official forums and social media web pages and be publicized in a well-organized manner.

5　Arranging Good Speakers and Trainers: The most important responsibility of Parent Academy leaders is to arrange impactful speakers. The best way to facilitate this opportunity is to announce and invite parents/guardians who hold interest or expertise in desired areas. For instance, a parent working in the field of nutrition can better conduct the seminar related to "Healthy Eating Habits." Similarly, a parent who is a dentist could be invited to conduct a session on "Dental Hygiene". A parent/guardian who has created a garden at home could give a workshop on how to start a home garden with your child. Parents can partner with other families; moreover, they can receive professional benefits by publicizing their profession, talents, and interests. They can also inspire others to opt for their profession.

Reflection Activity: Preservice Counselor in Training Reflects on First Attending School within the U.S. – by Ammal Mahmood

I was born and raised in Pakistan, and immigrated to Virginia, USA in 2002 with my family when I was seven years old. My mother changed my name to Ammal, meaning hope, because she came here full of hope, envisioning what we could be before. My parents wanted a better life for us, one that could give us opportunities to better ourselves. But they didn't know that all of our opportunities came with extra baggage: for every opportunity given, there were millions of people thinking they weren't deserved.

It became apparent to me early on that I didn't have anyone outside of my family to guide or mentor me. Being new immigrants, my family didn't have the resources to guide us or mentor us (other than to raise us to be good humans). Their entire focus was to provide us with our necessities: food and shelter. My parents were always scared. They didn't have the privilege to mess up. They thought everything would be stripped away. They knew we weren't welcome, but they still aimed to stabilize our family. There were language barriers, and our cultures were different. Despite the diversity at my school, I knew no one would understand my culture and the unique obstacles that we faced.

In primary school, I was held back in first grade because I didn't speak English. People subsequently bullied me because I was very tall for my age and grade. My teachers would yell at me for not answering them. I would get in trouble for my perceived transgressions (e.g., "I wasn't listening" or looked down as teachers spoke to me). In my culture, we weren't allowed to make eye contact with adults – an act considered disrespectful – but in America, avoiding eye contact is considered disrespectful by many teachers. After negotiating nuances and motions of acceptable behavior, it was time for third grade. In our school, there were a total of five third-grade teachers. The only Black teacher was considered to be the meanest of them all. I remember all my classmates wishing we weren't in her class because she "looked" mean. They made me think she was mean too, so I wished for the same. I held onto my mother as they were showing us our teachers and classrooms, and of course, she was my teacher: Mrs. Pamela Duke.

However, Mrs. Duke to this day is one of my *favorite* teachers. She was the first teacher who looked past any of my differences or weaknesses and believed in me. I never put my hand up or talked because I always doubted myself. I did not understand why I always got in trouble with other teachers, however, I tried my hardest academically and to be respectful toward everyone. Fortunately, Mrs. Duke broke the mold. Sometimes I would stay quiet and she would stay patient and urge me to try. If I did not participate, she would say, "Okay, next time." If I got answers wrong, she never belittled me or attributed it to me being dumb. She knew I just had some things to work on. And then she would take the time to work on them with me. She gave me a safe space to learn and be curious. I would tell everyone I met how she was nothing like they said. Rather, Mrs. Duke was the best teacher in the world. I wish I had her for every class. She even encouraged me to make friends. I only made two. One was a Hispanic girl, Susan, who constantly seemed annoyed at me and told me she hated me. I thought Susan was joking. I told her I loved her and she was my best friend. She would make a disgusted and annoyed face, as I proceeded to hug her, but then occasionally would smile. That was good enough for me!

My second friend was a Pakistani boy named Omar, who also had recently immigrated with his family to Virginia. Even as third graders, Omar and I spoke about the transition from our country of origin often. I would try to look out for him because he was always sleepy in class. I didn't want him to get in trouble for it. He came here with his dad and brother. His dad was always at work. His brother would often play games till the morning and skip school. His father was not around much. One day, despite my efforts to keep him awake, he fell asleep. I was scared. Mrs. Duke came and seemed disappointed; she took him to the side of the room and gave him a pillow and blanket, and told him to rest. She proceeded to teach the class as he slept. I was shocked. I said, "Are you going to hit him?" (I asked because within our culture spanking is a form of acceptable discipline.) And she said "No. It's not his fault. It's okay that he rests. When he wakes up we can tell him what he missed." I don't know what action she took behind the scenes, but that action in itself was enough to motivate Omar and me to be the best we could be in her class.

The next experience to share: Attending high school

We moved to different areas throughout my school life, and there were many challenges along the way. Throughout my elementary and middle school years, I did not know who my school counselors were. It was not until high school that I even spoke to one, and the sole purpose was to schedule my major and elective classes. I recall that all of the school counselors were White and all of the teachers were White, too. The racial diversity of the staff was evident with the teaching assistants, custodians, and maintenance staff. This lack of representation among the teaching faculty, school administrators, and other professionals within the school seemed normal. This lack of racial representation within schools remains. This lack of diversity that I noticed within high school made it difficult for me to transition well into a school where I felt I did not belong. I wanted to complete my course requirements and graduate from high school as quickly as possible. I set a goal to finish high school in three years, and I did it!! I did not want to be in a place where it appeared that even Black and Brown students wanted to be like the White kids, to be accepted and loved by them. It seemed like many of the students from racially diverse backgrounds denounced their cultural upbringing, saying things like they "hated their country of origin" or that they "hated their own people." We now know this is a form of internalized racism. Specifically in my experience, very few were proud of their racial heritage and many did not celebrate their cultural identities, and those who attempted to show pride were outcast. The students in the school formed cliques, and there was immense pressure to be perfect. I was able to make friends from different groups (e.g., cliques) within the school but because of the racial tension, these friendships never existed outside of the school. Hence, I never got the chance to have long-lasting meaningful relationships. So, I concentrated on my schoolwork and stacked up my classes to graduate as soon as possible.

That said, the highlight of my high school years was getting to know my World History teacher, Brian Miller. Mr. Miller was the first white teacher who seemed aware of other people's cultures and encouraged them. He caught me off guard multiple times in class. The first was when he pointed out to the class not to follow our history books *solely* because they are written by white old men who held firm to their biases and desired to only show positive aspects of a Eurocentric and Westernized ideology at any cost without illustrating a fuller objective perspective. And the second time was when we were discussing a chapter from our reading on terrorism. He said, "One country's terrorist is another country's hero." He said, "Do you think our soldiers are considered heroes in the countries they go and fight against?" He said, "No, so be mindful when you speak." He won my heart. *Not only did he block all the racist remarks in my class that were directed towards me being Muslim and unjustifiably connected to being a terrorist, but his remarks created an environment for us to think outside the box and welcome different perspectives.* He helped me with my academic and personal concerns, and this got me through high school. His guidance and support were tremendous because I thought I would never go to college because my family did not have the money. He took his lunch breaks to help show me the Free Application for Federal Student Aid (FAFSA) and other scholarships that I could apply to. He encouraged me and believed in me, and told me not to worry and to keep pushing forward. In my mind, he was more influential to me than any school counselor that I had. I committed to being a teacher like him one day. I was not familiar with the career path of a school counselor or mental health provider at the time.

I could not articulate clearly the lack of racial representation overall. However, I know how it impacted me upon reflection. These personal experiences motivate a call for SCs to be aware of the wide and varied perspectives of racially and culturally diverse schools. In addition to awareness, SCs must advocate to shed light on barriers and offer solutions to dismantle racist policies, procedures, and practices within school systems. I am one student. Imagine how many students before me and after me either had positive influences or surrendered to adversities. I was lucky, but not all students end up being that lucky. SCs can instill comprehensive and holistic roadmaps to improve the different systems our students go through.

Reflection prompt

It is important to note that adverse attitudes on behalf of school faculty and staffing will hamper strong school–family–community relationships.

Imagine that this preservice counselor is asked to create a school-family-community partnership with parents/guardians that focuses on developing student academic capabilities and empathy towards others within the learning environment. How might she work to bolster culturally responsive partnerships when facing biases and stereotypes of all sorts, regarding specific stakeholders or school partners?

Discussion Questions to Extend Learning

Given the fact that many school administrators do not have an accurate view of the role, appropriate functions, and relevant skills of their school counselors (Borders, 2002), consider the following:

1   How would you describe your role as a school counselor to a principal?
2   What venue would you use to present this information and what would you include in this discussion?
3   Would you include only school principals, or would you include other administrators from the central office? What about others from the community? Support your decision.

Summary

The school counseling field must recognize and challenge inequitable mental health, education, and social systems at every level in order to: a) address the needs of a child to help him or her to grow; b) understand one's identity as a school counselor and others in relation to their work; and c) be a positive personal and professional contributor in the larger society. Members of the school community and school counselors need to understand the importance of their respective roles. In turn, this understanding allows for mutual advocacy to provide comprehensive therapy and coordinated teaching that builds on students' support systems – their parents, extended family, friend networks, and trusted adults in the school community. In many cultures, it takes a village to raise a child. A school and its counselors are only one part of that village. A counselor can't support children alone.

Key Takeaways

1   Finding your passion or niche in school counseling doesn't need to be all-encompassing.
2   Advocacy and leadership come in many different forms.
3   The school counselor's identity is ever-evolving.

Chapter Application

1   Provide an application of consultation and collaboration that overlaps with supervision in school counseling.
2   The reader will consider how advocacy also necessitates that school counselors collaborate with and on behalf of minoritized students and families in school settings despite one's own racial, ethnic, and cultural backgrounds.

3 School counselors must see families as agentic partners to meet students' needs and developmental goals. An emphasis on early childhood and family collaboration is noted.

4 Conduct an online search of the American School Counseling Association Mindsets and Behaviors. Jot down the strengths and areas of improvement on these concepts. Think about those that you would feel comfortable teaching to the young people within your family. Examine those mindsets and behaviors that you would be less comfortable instilling in them.

5 What about you personally? Which mindsets and behaviors might you be cautious about when working with Black and Brown students? Are any of them punitive or controlling? To what extent should we even be attempting to alter one's mindset or behavior within a school setting?

References

American School Counselor Association (2019). *ASCA national model: A Framework for school counseling programs* (4th ed.). Author

Bryan, J., & Henry, L. (2008). Strengths-based partnerships: A school-family-community partnership approach to empowering students. *Professional School Counseling, 12*, 149–156.

Bryan, J. A., & Griffin, D. (2010). A multidimensional study of school-family-community partnership involvement: School, school counselor, and training factors. *Professional School Counseling, 14*(1), 75–86.

Bryan, J., Moore-Thomas, C., Day-Vines, N. L., & Holcomb-McCoy, C. (2011). School counselors as social capital: The effects of high school college counseling on college application rates. *Journal of Counseling & Development, 89*(2), 190–199.

Bryan, J., & Henry, L. (2012). A model for building school-family-community partnerships: Principles and process. *Journal of Counseling & Development, 90*(4), 408–420.

Bryan, J., Griffin, D., Kim, J., Griffin, D. M., & Young, A. (2019). School counselor leadership in school-family-community partnerships: An equity-focused partnership process model for moving the field forward. *The Wiley handbook on family, school, and community relationships in education*, 265–287.

Borders, L. D. (2002). School counseling in the 21st century: Personal and professional reflections. *Professional School Counseling, 5*, 180–185.

Gysbers, N. C., & Henderson, P. (2014). *Developing and managing your school guidance and counseling program.* John Wiley & Sons.

Holcomb-McCoy, C., Ileana, G., & Georgina, J. (2009). School counselor dispositions as predictors of data usage. *Professional School Counseling, 12*(5), 343–351.

Holcomb-McCoy, C., & Bryan, J. (2010). Advocacy and empowerment in parent consultation: Implications for theory and practice. *Journal of Counseling & Development, 88*(3), 259–268.

Johnson, J., Rochkind, J., & Ott, A. (2010). Why guidance counseling needs to change. *Educational Leadership, 67*(7), 74–79.

McDonough, P. M. (2005). Counseling and college counseling in America's high schools. *State of college admission,* 107–121.

Mitchell, M. M., & Bradshaw, C. P. (2013). Examining classroom influences on student perceptions of school climate: The role of classroom management and exclusionary discipline strategies. *Journal of School Psychology, 51*(5), 599–610.

Posey-Maddox, L. (2017). Race in place: Black parents, family-school relations, and multispatial microaggressions in a predominantly White suburb (EJ1143661). *Teachers College Record, 119*(12), 1–42.

Trusty, J., & Brown, D. (2005). Advocacy competencies for professional school counselors. *Professional School Counseling,* 259–265.

United States. Office of Educational Research, Improvement. Center for Education Statistics, & Institute of Education Sciences (US). (2010). *Digest of education statistics* (Vol. 46). US Department of Health, Education, and Welfare, Education Division, National Center for Education Statistics.

Whiston, S. C. (1996). Accountability through action research: Research methods for practitioners. *Journal of Counseling & Development, 74*(6), 616–623.

Young, A. A., & Bryan, J. A. (2018). The school counselor leadership survey: Confirmatory factor analysis and validation. *Measurement and Evaluation in Counseling and Development, 51*(4), 235–249.

Young, A., & Kaffenberger, C. (2011). The beliefs and practices of school counselors who use data to implement comprehensive school counseling programs. *Professional School Counseling, 15*(2), 67–76. Retrieved from https://search-proquest-com.mutex.gmu.edu/scholarly-journals/beliefs-practices-school-counselors-who-use-data/docview/912754318/se-2?accountid=14541

Zandi, M. (2009). The economic impact of the American Recovery and Reinvestment Act. *Report. January, 21,* 1–18.

Chapter 8

Neurodiversity and Exceptional Children

Key Terms (See Chapter 1)
504 plan, Adverse Childhood Experiences (Aces). The Americans with Disabilities Act (ADA), Individualized Education Plan, Racial/Ethnic Disproportionality, Significant Disproportionality

Author Narrative: Shekila Melchior

In my first year as a school counselor, I was wholly unprepared for an encounter I had with a student. The student entered my office in distress wanting to know if I could help her and also if she could go to the nurse for a cut on her wrist. When I asked how I could help, the student told me that the night before she kept seeing things and was afraid someone was coming to get her. Thinking she was asleep, she slit her wrists "in the dream" to wake up. She quickly realized that she was not asleep and had slit her wrists. As a first-year school counselor, I was overwhelmed, scared, and at a loss for what to do next. I understood that a referral was the next necessary step, but a referral to where? The hospital? A community clinic? I also had very little knowledge of the *Diagnostic and Statistical Manual of Mental Disorders* (DSM). This experience taught me that while I do not diagnose as a school counselor, a strong working knowledge of the DSM would have decreased my fears and provided me with more clarity on the best referral route.

Content

The term "significant disproportionality" is used to describe the widespread trend of students of certain racial and ethnic groups being identified for special education, placed in more restrictive educational settings, and disciplined at markedly higher rates than their peers. Due to bias within the education system (including within assessments and academic and other policies), Black and Brown students can be misidentified as needing

DOI: 10.4324/9781003226253-10

special education, and are then placed in more restrictive settings and experience harsher discipline because of the intersectionality of race and special education – all of which can negatively affect student outcomes. Educational professionals and policymakers must understand the magnitude of significant disproportionality for students of different races and ethnicities and take action to correct it and prevent it from happening.

Exceptional Children

School counselors are qualified mental health professionals who are trained to work with a myriad of mental health disorders in a brief, time-limited, and team-oriented approach. School counselors' scope of work often focuses on depression, anxiety, attachment and conduct disorders, substance misuse, and learning and intellectual disabilities. Children who experience severe mental illness are rare, representing less than 5% of the total child and adolescent population with mental illness. The following sections will explore common diagnoses in children and brief overviews of the IDEA Act (2004), Individualized Education Plan (2000), and 504 Plan (1978). In addition to an overview, we will examine the role of the school counselor in collaboration with stakeholders such as special education teachers and outside treatment providers. Finally, we will explore the misdiagnosis of racial-ethnic minority children and the detrimental contributions it has on a child's future.

The Role of the School Counselor

The school counselor plays a significant role in the support of students with disabilities. School counselors serve as referral resources for stakeholders in the school building and oftentimes are members of the interdisciplinary team that serves the needs of students with disabilities. School counselors can also provide counseling support, offering students coping skills, assistance with academic work, and familial support and encouragement. School counselors also work in collaboration with various stakeholders such as mental health agency professionals, school psychologists, social workers, faculty, and staff to ensure the needs of all students with disabilities are served.

The school counseling field must contend with the ways in which sociohistorical conditions influence outcomes for school counseling professionals, school partners, and the institutions in which they are situated. More work is needed to acknowledge the role of *social stratification* (García Coll et al., 1996; Perez-Brena et al., 2018) in shaping adverse childhood experiences (ACEs) outside of school, adaptive and positive coping mechanisms, and learning in schools at the macrosystems level (Shonkoff et al., 2012).

Diagnosis in Children

Common Statistics

The most common diagnoses found in children are anxiety/depression, behavioral problems, and ADHD. According to the CDC (2023), among children ages 3–17, 9.8% (6.0 million) have ADHD; 9.4% (5.8 million) have anxiety; 8.9% (5.5 million) have behavior problems; and 4.4% (2.7 million) have depression. Anxiety and depression have increased over time. Substance misuse and suicide are areas of concern: 4.4% of adolescents have been diagnosed with a substance misuse disorder, 1.6% alcohol use, and 3.2% illicit drug use. In addition, 18.8% have seriously considered attempting suicide; 15.7% made a suicide plan; 8.9% attempted suicide, and 2.5% made a suicide attempt that required medical treatment. One in six children between two and eight years old (17.4%) has a mental, behavioral, or developmental disorder. Moreover, Adverse Childhood Events (ACEs) are associated with the physical and mental health of the child. Research also indicates that racial/ethnic minoritized children who experienced discrimination indicate a higher percentage of one or more physical (37.8%) and/or mental health (27.1%) conditions. The diagnostic categories are disruptive behavior disorders, neurodevelopmental (neurodivergent) disorders, eating disorders, mood disorders and anxiety, schizophrenia spectrum and psychotic disorders (rare), and trauma and stressor-related disorders. A brief overview of each diagnostic category is provided.

Disruptive Behavior Disorders

Several factors contribute to the high incidence of emotional disturbance in children. Research has indicated that environmental factors related to family breakdown, poverty, witnessing violence, and homelessness can contribute to emotional disturbance. Other factors can include limited access to mental health services, poor health insurance, and lack of transportation. These factors, however, can contribute to other disorders as well. The lack of access to mental health services is a pervasive problem that contributes to an ever-growing crisis of mental health issues. In addition, the lack of access in underrepresented communities can lead to an overrepresentation in special education programs, a misdiagnosis, or limited care. Further exploration of the misdiagnosis and overrepresentation of underrepresented communities is presented later in the chapter. There are two categories that the *Diagnostic Statistical Manual V-TR** (DSM-V-TR) (APA, 2022) identifies as disruptive behavior disorders: conduct disorder and oppositional disorder. Individuals with a conduct disorder are often aggressive against people and animals, destroy property, are deceitful, and often violate rules. Children with oppositional disorders have a pattern of negative, hostile, and defiant behaviors that last at least six months. They often lose their temper, are argumentative, and refuse to comply. *Support for children who have disruptive behavior disorders could include individual counseling, intervention with the family, and interventions at the school level, such as Response to Intervention (*RTI), *likely Tier III.* The RTI (see appendix for image) is a tiered approach to service offered to students. Tier I comprises services provided for all students; Tier II is for students who fail to respond to Tier I interventions (about 15% of the student population); and Tier III is for students who fail to respond to Tier II interventions and need more individualized support (about 5% of the student population).

Neurodivergent Disorders

Neurodevelopmental disorders, now expressed as Neurodivergent disorders, encompass Autism spectrum disorder (ASD), Intellectual Development Disorders, and Attention Deficit/Hyperactivity Disorder (ADHD). ASD is defined by the DSM as having an impairment of social behavior and communication as well as abnormalities of what is considered routine behavior (APA, 2022). Additional criteria include flat affect, minimal social speech, poor eye contact, repetitive body movement, disinterested attention from parents or peers, rare engagements in play, and language impairment. The DSM V-TR provides the following criteria for Intellectual development disorders: the onset of the disorder is prior to age 18 and is often diagnosed in infancy or early childhood; 25–30% are biological cases. If an individual has a mild case, then the disorder is often diagnosed during school age. The criteria also include a diagnosis of sub-average intellectual functioning, and impaired adaptive functioning in at least two areas (communication, social skills, interpersonal skills, self-direction, leisure, functional academic skills, safety, and work). Lastly, the DSM divides ADHD into two parts: a presentation that is predominantly hyperactive-impulsive and a presentation that is predominantly inattentive. An individual can receive a diagnosis of both.

Disordered Eating

Disordered eating is divided into four diagnoses, pica, rumination, anorexia-nervosa, and bulimia. Pica is the ingesting of non-food substances and is commonly linked to children with an intellectual development disorder and/ or an autism spectrum disorder. Rumination is when an individual often regurgitates or re-chews their food, this can also be linked to children with an intellectual development disorder and/or an autism spectrum disorder. Anorexia nervosa occurs when an individual is below normal weight, has a fear of gaining weight, and has a disturbed body image. Finally, bulimia is characterized as binge eating with vomiting, fasting, or extreme exercise and lasts at least three months. Some individuals may binge eat without the above-mentioned criteria or restrict their eating.

Mood Disorders and Anxiety

Mood Disorders and anxiety are two of the most common diagnoses seen in children, and often show up differently in adults. Depression is categorized as five or more symptoms being present for two weeks or more, with at least one of the symptoms being a depressed mood or loss of interest. These symptoms should occur daily. The DSM endorses six types of depression: major depression, persistent depressive disorder (dysthymia), melancholic, psychotic, seasonal affective disorder (SAD), and premenstrual dysphoric disorder. Major depression is a severe depression that is long-lasting and significantly impairs an individual's daily functioning. Dysthymia is chronic and low-grade, can get better or worse over time, and lasts for at least two years. Melancholic is a severe form in which there are persistent feelings of extreme hopelessness and sadness. Individuals who are depressed with psychotic features have a severe form of depression accompanied by hallucinations and/or delusions. SAD is characterized as a cyclical disorder that intermittently appears as the seasons change. Lastly, premenstrual dysphoric disorder is an extreme premenstrual syndrome that can lead to intense and debilitating mood shifts.

Anxiety is categorized as either separation anxiety; additional distress upon separation; or generalized anxiety, which includes worried or anxious feelings about many aspects of life. Generalized anxiety can manifest physical symptoms. Two additional mood disorders are Bipolar I and Bipolar II. Bipolar I is categorized by manic and depressive episodes, whereas Bipolar II is categorized by one or more major depressive disorders and at least one manic episode.

Schizophrenia Spectrum and Psychotic Disorders

Schizophrenia spectrum and psychotic disorders in children are rare. The average age of onset is 18–24; 1 in 10,000 children are diagnosed with schizophrenia. Symptoms of schizophrenia and psychosis are flat affect, social withdrawal, inattention, impulsivity, hallucinations (audio, visual, or tactile), delusion, and illogical conversations and thought patterns.

Trauma and Stressor-Related Disorders

Trauma can be defined as something that overwhelms a person's system. It can, for example, be something that happens too much too soon or not enough. It can be a single incident or chronic. Trauma could be a car accident; physical, emotional, or sexual abuse; or race-based trauma, to name a few. The diagnostic criteria for trauma and stress-related disorders are characterized by symptoms that cause "clinically significant distress or impairment" to the individual's functioning.

Overview of Special Education Services

The Americans with Disabilities Act (ADA) is federal disability anti-discrimination legislation passed in 1990. The ADA guaranteed rights to individuals with disabilities in the areas of employment, transportation, government services, telecommunication, and public accommodations (ADA, 1990). Before ADA and the IDEA, Section 504 of the Vocational Rehabilitation Act was passed in 1973. This legislation is similar to the IDEA Act. The Individuals with Disabilities Education Act (IDEA) was also passed in 1990 and guaranteed students with disabilities the right to free appropriate education in the least restrictive environment. There are 14 areas that the IDEA recognizes as eligible disorders; these areas are broadly defined and placed within clusters. A learning disability is a disorder characterized by a child's difficulty or a delay in the development of their ability to learn. An emotional or behavioral disorder is characterized by disruptive or inappropriate behaviors. Intellectual disabilities are characterized by deficits in adaptive functioning and significant intellectual impairment. Lastly, autism spectrum disorder is defined as a developmental disability that may result in significant delay and developmental differences. The identification process, as addressed by the IDEA, is a mandate to find and identify all students with a disability from birth to 21 years of age. In an effort to do so, each school has a school-based identification team of interdisciplinary stakeholders that review the academic achievement, social-emotional and cognitive ability of the child. The team may also utilize standardized testing (e.g., WISC-IV & WIAT-II) to measure academic achievement and intellectual functioning to identify learning disabilities.

A decision is rendered and the child may receive a 504 Plan or an Individualized Education Plan (IEP), or be deemed as not having a disability – or at least not a disability that would impact the student's progress (2000). For a child to be eligible for a 504 Plan, they must present documentation of a disability (or disabilities) that significantly limits their performance and life activities (Departmnet of Health, Education, and Welfare, 1978). Students who are deemed eligible are provided a 504 Plan that outlines accommodations and modifications necessary for the student to perform life activities and attend school with their peers . It is important to note that the 504 Plan can be temporary. The IEP, while similar to a 504 Plan, is more extensive. The IEP is used to describe the student's current level of development and their learning goals. Each student with an IEP is given a multidisciplinary IEP team that develops and evaluates the IEP in concert with the parent/guardian and student. As the student transitions out of services they receive an Individualized Transition Plan, which outlines the services needed as the student enters adulthood. Students who receive special education services and support may receive accommodations, providing the student access (i.e., extended time) while still educating them from a general education curriculum that remains unchanged. Modifications, however, fundamentally change the content of the curriculum to provide students with support. Students with disabilities may also receive other related services from professionals within their community to help meet their needs.

Adverse Childhood Experiences (ACEs)

Adverse Childhood Experiences (ACEs) was a longitudinal study conducted in 1995–1997 examining the following factors:

- Economic hardship
- Divorce or separation of a parent
- Death of a parent
- Incarcerated parent
- Witness to adult domestic violence
- Victim or witness to neighborhood violence
- Household member who is mentally ill or suicidal
- Household member who is an alcohol or substance abuser
- Race/ethnicity discrimination

ACEs are potentially traumatic events occurring during childhood (0–17). The impact of these events is linked to mental illness, substance misuse, and chronic health problems. ACEs are common, and some children are at a greater risk of ACEs than others (Felitti et al., 1998). Since the completion of the study, significant literature has contributed to the prevention of ACEs and the treatment of children who have experienced the events listed above (Table 8.1).

Table 8.1 Challenges and Barriers Addressing ACEs

Challenges and Barriers		
School level policies	Course placement	Discipline policies
Participation restriction	Gatekeepers to AP courses	Unfair suspension practices
Withholding participation for fees	Who is actively working to remove barriers	Zero tolerance policies
Unfair practices with English-language learners and differently-abled or neurodivergent individuals	Role of adults and other stakeholders	Alternatives to suspension

Disproportionality in Special Education

"Significant disproportionality" refers to three separate but related trends that impact a student's educational experience: (1) identification for special education (also called eligibility); (2) educational placement (once identified as eligible for special education); and (3) discipline. The connection between the overdiagnosis of Black children and the prison industrial complex is startling, and Black children are 40% more likely to be identified than other students. Contrarily, some researchers believe that racial/ethnic minoritized children have higher rates of disability and are underrepresented as a result of a lack of access. Taking an intersectional approach, the support of this theory is the connection to poverty, which serves as a risk factor for disability. Moreover, connections have been made between ACEs and a child's diagnosis. While it is important to review many perspectives on disproportionality, there is overwhelming research on how systemic racism contributes to the over-representation of racial/ethnically minoritized. Research has shown that Black and Hispanic students who are from non-low-income backgrounds are more likely to be diagnosed with an intellectual disability or emotional disturbance compared with their White peers. NCLD offers an intriguing hypothesis: disabilities that are objective (vision or hearing) have a clear root cause, whereas subjective disabilities, "depend on the professional judgment – and potentially the biases – of the assessors" (NCLD, 2020, P.4). More subjective disabilities are specific learning disabilities, intellectual disabilities, and emotional disturbance. Additionally, a misdiagnosis can impact the student's academic trajectory by placing them in less-rigorous courses. The expectations may be lower, thus diminishing their postsecondary education opportunities. Aside from academics, misidentification can have negative consequences for their well-being, lower self-esteem, increase exposure to stigma, and significantly reduce their opportunity to make the transition out of special education services, despite being misdiagnosed.

The IDEA act encourages schools to place children in the least restrictive environment, encouraging schools to place students in general education classrooms, often with the support of an inclusion teacher. While more than 80% of students with disabilities are in general education classrooms, 33% of Black students spend their day in general education classrooms compared to 55% of their White peers. This disparity further widens the achievement gap of Black students – a gap that further exacerbates the systemic racism that persists in K-12 schools.

Lastly, the overrepresentation and misidentification of racial/ethnic minority students are directly correlated to racial/ethnic disproportionality of discipline rates in school, resulting in an increase of punitive measures in k-12 school settings contributing to mass incarceration and the negative impact on the student's academic performance and overall well-being

(Nishioka et al., 2017). Black, Hispanic/Latine students are more likely to receive harsher punishments, referrals, suspensions, and expulsions. Black students specifically are suspended or expelled three times the rate of their White peers. Consequently, the suspension and expulsion rates for students with disabilities are even higher. One in four racial/ethnic minority boys and one in five racial/ethnic minority girls receive out-of-school suspension. Black males are suspended at the highest rate of all groups. Research has further explored the restraining of students in school, which happens more frequently to students with disabilities, especially Black students. While Black students only make up 19% of students with disabilities, studies report that they make up 36% of students with disabilities who are restrained, physically or mechanically. Physical restraint, performed by an adult, decreases the child's ability to move freely. Mechanical restraint is the use of a device to restrict the ability to move freely. The issue of restraint bears a startling correlation between restraint and police brutality against racial/ethnic minorities. NAMI said, "Almost half the people who die at the hands of police have some kind of disability." (NCLD, 2020)

Collaboration

Special educators and school counselors are trained to be culturally competent providers who are knowledgeable about the unique systemic barriers that minoritized students with learning disabilities face. Efforts have been made to address disproportionality and to offer recommendations for reducing disproportionality. Collaborative advocacy efforts between special education teachers and counselors are necessary to address these issues.

Summary

School Counselors, educational leaders, researchers and policymakers can help shine a light on significant disproportionality for students of different races and ethnicities. Motivated and action-oriented educational professionals can make a difference by proactively and intentionally addressing discrepancies and cultivating environments that prevent these injustices from happening in the first place.

Reflection Questions

In groups, consider the following prompts:

1 Can you think of students who are never allowed to participate in special classes, teams, or school activities due to discipline referrals or behavioral concerns?

2 What race are most of the children you are thinking of? What gender? Can these children map a path to success? Are they ever caught being good? Can you think of adults who are "in their corner"?
3 What is the racial makeup of special education courses in your school? Have you participated in conversations in IEP eligibility meetings or special education meetings on the overrepresentation and disproportionality of racial/ethnic minorities in special education?

Key Takeaways

1 While school counselors don't diagnose, it is vital to have a strong understanding of the DSM as a resource.
2 One must recognize the bias related to the DSM when it comes to diagnosing.
3 School counselors need to advocate on behalf of, and with, students to ensure that appropriate services are offered to the students.

Chapter Application

1 Review the author narrative provided by Shekila at the beginning of this chapter. What would you do if you were in this situation? What if the student sent you a text message relating the same information and it is after school hours? In any event, at this point of your learning, what role does the diagnosis play in your decision-making for the child? What additional areas of learning do you need to access?
2 Discuss personal examples that the reader may have had concerning this topic. What were these experiences? If they were not positive, how would one ensure that this does not happen to other students and families?

References

A Guide to the Individualized Education Program. (2000). [Washington, DC]: Office of Special Education and Rehabilitative Services, U.S. Dept. of Education: Office of Educational Research and Improvement, Educational Resources Information Center,

Americans With Disabilities Act of 1990, 42 U.S.C. § 12101 *et seq.* (1990).

American Psychiatric Association. (2022). *Diagnostic and statistical manual of mental disorders* (5th ed., text rev.). 10.1176/appi.books.9780890425787

Centers for Disease Control and Prevention. (2023, March 8). *Data and statistics on children's mental health.* Centers for Disease Control and Prevention. Retrieved April 14, 2023, from https://www.cdc.gov/childrensmentalhealth/data.html

Coll, C. G., Crnic, K., Lamberty, G., Wasik, B. H., Jenkins, R., Garcia, H. V., &

McAdoo, H. P. (1996). An integrative model for the study of developmental competencies in minority children. *Child development, 67*(5), 1891–1914.

Felitti, V. J., Anda, R. F., Nordenberg, D., & Williamson, D. F. (1998). Adverse childhood experiences and health outcomes in adults: The Ace study. *Journal of Family and Consumer Sciences, 90*(3), 31.

Individuals With Disabilities Education Act, 20 U.S.C. § 1400 (2004).

National Center for Education Statistics. (2022). Students With disabilities. *Condition of education.* U.S. Department of Education, Institute of Education Sciences. Retrieved [date], from https://nces.ed.gov/programs/coe/indicator/cgg.

National Center for Learning Disabilities. (2020). Significant Disproportionality in Special Education: Trends Among Black Students. Retrieved March 1, 2023, from https://www.ncld.org/wp-content/uploads/2020/10/2020-NCLD-Disproportionality_-English-Learners_EL_FINAL.pdf

Nishioka, V., Shigeoka, S., & Lolich, E. (2017). *School discipline data indicators: A guide for districts and schools (REL 2017–240).* Washington, DC: U.S. Department of Education, Institute of Education Sciences, National Center for Education Evaluation and Regional Assistance, Regional Educational Laboratory Northwest. http://ies.ed.gov/ncee/edlabs.

Perez-Brena, N. J., Rivas-Drake, D., Toomey, R. B., & Umaña-Taylor, A. J. (2018). Contributions of the integrative model for the study of developmental competencies in minority children: What have we learned about adaptive culture? *American Psychologist, 73*(6), 713.

Shonkoff, J. P., Garner, A. S., Committee on Psychosocial Aspects of Child and Family Health, Committee on Early Childhood, Adoption, and Dependent Care, and Section on Developmental and Behavioral Pediatrics, Siegel, B. S., Dobbins, M. I., Earls, M. F., ... & Wood, D. L. (2012). The lifelong effects of early childhood adversity and toxic stress. *Pediatrics, 129*(1), e232–e246

United States. Department of Health, Education, and Welfare. Office for Civil Rights. (1978). Section 504 of the Rehabilitation Act of 1973: fact sheet: handicapped persons rights under Federal law. Washington: Dept. of Health, Education, and Welfare, Office of the Secretary, Office for Civil Rights

Ziomek-Daigle, J., Goodman-Scott, E., Cavin, J., & Donohue, P. (2016). Integrating a multi-tiered system of supports with comprehensive school counseling programs. *The Professional Counselor, 6*, 220–232.

Chapter 9

Culturally Sustaining Ethical School Counseling Practice

Author Narrative: Sam Steen

One day at work a young, Black boy in the second grade was brought to my office by a teacher because of a bruise on his ear. After exploring with the student what could have caused this bruise, it was stated that he had been burned by his mother. Oh, My Goodness!! He's been burned by his mother. Could this be abuse? Was he also being neglected daily? He was an African American boy living in a middle-class neighborhood; however, I may have assumed his family was considered to be from a low-income background because everything I had read about Black youth was negative. I was stressed. So, without much consultation with anyone I decided to call Child Protective Services (CPS). I honestly do not remember if I asked the principal or not, but regardless, I sent the student back to class, called CPS, and don't remember much else from that day. CPS has a policy that after you make the call, you may not hear anything back, as it is no longer in your hands. Whether or not they follow up may never be disclosed, as it is not imperative that they share findings or anything that comes from the report.

However, the next day as I was entering work, I heard a mother entering the school and seeking the administration to find *"Mr. Steen."* Soon, I was called down to the office. The mother of the second-grader confronted me directly and curtly. She was livid. Following this terse introduction, she asked the young boy to speak and share what happened to him. He shared at that moment that he was playing with his mom's curling iron and that she had warned him about the risk. The mother then addressed me again and said, "Sir, you need to understand something. Every little Black child you are working with is not living in a family that is in danger." She continued by saying, "I would hope that you as a Black man would know better."

I learned many valuable lessons at this stage of my career. The lessons can be summed up as follows: (1) it is important to build relationships with families through open communication so that when challenged to decide on issues of abuse you can be confident that you are not discriminating

DOI: 10.4324/9781003226253-11

based on personal biases; (2) it is important to consult with others to get a wider perspective and more feedback on what could be happening in the situation; (3) it is important to err on the side of caution when handling these dilemmas; (4) acts of systemic racism and oppressive school environments are not perpetuated only by White people; and (5) Black professionals and other minoritized communities may carry internalized racism that needs to be exposed and combatted regularly.

Content

CACREP

To stimulate an understanding of the CACREP School Counseling Specialty Standard that addresses "legal and ethical" considerations, this simple statement is an area that budding and seasoned school counselors alike should understand and/or apply:

> School counselors must be knowledgeable and able to readily apply "Legal and ethical considerations specific to school counseling" within their work.

Reflection One

Consider the following prompts in groups:

1 When reflecting upon this statement, what stands out to you?
2 What does it mean, in your opinion?
3 Why is the term "legal" included?
4 How should one go about their daily interactions within schools and communities where they work?
5 Within your counselor training program, what messages around legal and ethical considerations emerged when preparing you to be an equity-focused school counseling professional?

Selected ACA Code of Ethics Examples

Below we continue exploring legal and ethical standards as espoused by the American Counseling Association, which may not necessarily differentiate legal and ethical considerations for school counselors but could shed light on the role and function of a legally and ethically sound counselor.

The ACA Code of Ethics defines multicultural/diversity counseling within the glossary as follows:

Multicultural/Diversity Counseling – counseling that recognizes diversity and embraces approaches that support the worth, dignity, potential, and uniqueness of individuals within their historical, cultural, economic, political, and psychosocial contexts.

The ACA Code of Ethics defines social justice within the glossary as follows:

Social Justice – the promotion of equity for all people and groups for the purpose of ending oppression and injustice affecting clients, students, counselors, families, communities, schools, workplaces, governments, and other social and institutional systems.

This document highlights how to use the ACA ethical guidelines:

The introductions help set the tone for each particular section and provide a starting point that invites reflection on the ethical standards contained in each part of the ACA Code of Ethics.

The purpose of the statement above is to give some direction as to why this information is presented in this way.

Following are more thorough comments that shed light on the ambiguity that accompanies every single situation/scenario. It is important to remember that nothing is as clear as one would hope. This work is difficult, and helping others achieve their personal goals comes with the potential harm that underlies every counseling interaction.

The standards outline professional responsibilities and provide direction for fulfilling those ethical responsibilities. When counselors are faced with ethical dilemmas that are difficult to resolve, they are expected to engage in a carefully considered ethical decision-making process, consulting available resources as needed. Counselors acknowledge that resolving ethical issues is a process; ethical reasoning includes consideration of professional values, professional ethical principles, and ethical standards.

To make this exercise of examining the ACA Ethical Codes more manageable and relevant to school counselors, some of the sections within this code address issues related indirectly to a school context. When possible at least one example is provided for each section below to give some direction and provide a platform for you to become familiar with the overlap of the ACA Ethical Codes with the school counseling profession.

Section A: The Counseling Relationship

A.7.a. Advocacy. When appropriate, counselors (e.g., school counselors) advocate at individual, group, institutional, and societal levels to address potential barriers and obstacles that inhibit access and/or the growth and development of clients.

Section B: Confidentiality and Privacy

B.5.b. Responsibility to Parents and Legal Guardians. Counselors inform parents and legal guardians about the role of counselors and the confidential nature of the counseling relationship, consistent with current legal and custodial arrangements. Counselors are sensitive to the cultural diversity of families and respect the inherent rights and responsibilities of parents/guardians regarding the welfare of their children/charges according to the law. Counselors work to establish, as appropriate, collaborative relationships with parents/guardians to best serve clients.

Section C: Professional Responsibility

C.2.a. Boundaries of Competence. Counselors practice only within the boundaries of their competence, based on their education, training, supervised experience, state and national professional credentials, and appropriate professional experience. Whereas multicultural counseling competency is required across all counseling specialties, counselors gain knowledge, personal awareness, sensitivity, dispositions, and skills pertinent to being a culturally competent counselor working with a diverse client population.

Section D: Relationships With Other Professionals

D.1.e. Confidentiality. When counselors are required by law, institutional policy, or extraordinary circumstances to serve in more than one role in judicial or administrative proceedings, they clarify role expectations and the parameters of confidentiality with their colleagues.

Section E: Evaluation, Assessment, and Interpretation

E.3.a. Explanation to Clients. Prior to an assessment, counselors explain the nature and purposes of the assessment and the specific use of results by potential recipients. The explanation will be given in terms and language that the client (or another legally authorized person on behalf of the client) can understand.

Section F: Supervision, Training, and Teaching

No clear connection could be made.

Section G: Research and Publication

G.2.c. Client Participation. Counselors conducting research involving clients make clear in the informed consent process that clients are free to choose whether to participate in research activities. Counselors take necessary precautions to protect clients from adverse consequences of declining or withdrawing from participation.

Section H: Distance Counseling, Technology, and Social Media

H.6.a. Virtual Professional Presence. In cases where counselors wish to maintain a professional and personal presence for social media use, separate professional and personal web pages and profiles are created to clearly distinguish between the two kinds of virtual presence.

Section I: Resolving Ethical Issues

I.2.b. Reporting Ethical Violations. If an apparent violation has substantially harmed or is likely to substantially harm a person or organization and is not appropriate for informal resolution or is not resolved properly, counselors take further action depending on the situation. Such action may include referral to state or national committees on professional ethics, voluntary national certification bodies, state licensing boards, or appropriate institutional authorities. The confidentiality rights of clients should be considered in all actions. This standard does not apply when counselors have been retained to review the work of another counselor whose professional conduct is in question (e.g., consultation, expert testimony).

Reflection Two

As you reviewed the ACA Ethical Codes that have been extrapolated to make a connection to school counselors, students, families, and school professional colleagues, take a moment to jot down a few thoughts, feelings, or reactions to this information. Next, take some more time to think through the questions below. If possible, share your reflections with your peers, colleagues, professor, or supervisors, as appropriate.

1   In your experience at this point, how relevant to school counselors is the ACA Code of Ethics?

2 How do you envision consulting this document if you find yourself and/ or your colleagues involved in situations involving legal and/or ethical violations?

3 What is the biggest insight gained when reviewing these samples and language within the ACA Code of Ethics?

4 What aspects of the ACA Code of Ethics could be improved?

5 As an equity-focused school counselor, how do you communicate to others that you also function in a legally and ethically sound manner?

6 When you encounter colleagues who are not fostering environments that offer an opportunity for students, parents/guardians, or others to thrive, what is the first thing you will do?

Selected ASCA Ethical Standards

Below we shift to the American School Counseling Association (ASCA) Ethical Standards. The main goal of these standards is to give school counselors a resource for applying "the principles of ethical behavior necessary to maintain the high standards of integrity, leadership and professionalism" (ASCA, 2016, page 1). While some would argue that the ASCA ethical guidelines offer "a deep understanding of cultural competency, equity, and social justice for school counselors" (Atkins & Oglesby, 2018, pg 35), there is much room for improvement from our vantage point. Use a lens of equity and inclusion when reviewing the ASCA ethical standards extrapolated below and determine whether you have gained a deeper understanding to engage in a fight for equity and access for the communities you will serve.

As we begin exploring a more relevant document, the purpose of the ASCA Ethical Standards is to offer:

• A guide for ethical practices of all school counselors, supervisors/ directors of school counseling programs, and school counselor educators regardless of level, area, population served, or membership in this professional association;

• Support and direction for self-assessment, peer consultation, and evaluations regarding school counselors' responsibilities to students, parents/guardians, colleagues and professional associates, schools district employees, communities, and the school counseling profession; and

• Insight to all stakeholders, including students, parents/guardians, teachers, administrators, community members, and courts of justice of best ethical practices, values, and expected behaviors of the school counseling professional (ASCA, 2016, pg 1).

Due to the explicit and direct focus on school counselors, the aspects of these ethical standards are examined to the extent to which they include cultural considerations (e.g., race, ethnicity, gender, class, spirituality, ability, and so forth). Within this document, there are six sections:

1 Responsibility to students;
2 Responsibilities to parents/guardians, to school, and self;
3 School counselor administrators/supervisors;
4 School counseling intern site supervisors;
5 Maintenance of standards; and
6 Ethical decision-making.

Within each of these sections is plenty of information that school counselors should know, should do, and should avoid. The last section, Ethical Decision Making suggests that, if/when faced with an ethical dilemma, school counselors and colleagues use a decision-making model. We attempt to provide as many examples of our aspirations for the ASCA Ethical Standards to lead the profession in an equity-focused manner.

Responsibility to Students

When school counselors are supporting student development they must "respect students' and families' values, beliefs, sexual orientation, gender identification/expression, and cultural background and exercise great care to avoid imposing personal beliefs or values rooted in one's religion, culture, or ethnicity."

Regarding confidentiality, school counselors must:

> inform students of the purposes, goals, techniques, and rules of procedure under which they may receive counseling. Disclosure includes informed consent and clarification of the limits of confidentiality. Informed consent requires competence, voluntariness, and knowledge on the part of students to understand the limits of confidentiality and, therefore, can be difficult to obtain from students of certain developmental levels, English-language learners, and special-needs populations. If the student can give assent/consent before school counselors share confidential information, school counselors attempt to gain the student's assent/consent.

School counselors who create and facilitate comprehensive data-informed programs must "review school and student data to assess needs including, but not limited to, data on disparities that may exist related to gender, race, ethnicity, socio-economic status, and/or other relevant classifications."

School counselors helping along the lines of academic, career, and social/emotional plans "identify gaps in college and career access and the implications of such data for addressing both intentional and unintentional biases related to college and career counseling."

When school counselors desire to make appropriate referrals and advocacy, they:

- Refrain from referring students based solely on the school counselor's personal beliefs or values rooted in one's religion, culture, ethnicity, or personal worldview.
- Maintain the highest respect for student diversity.
- Pursue additional training and supervision in areas where they are at risk of imposing their values on students, especially when the school counselor's values are discriminatory.
- Not impose their values on students and/or families when making referrals to outside resources for student and/or family support.

School counselors who provide support to underserved and at-risk populations:

- Strive to contribute to a safe, respectful, nondiscriminatory school environment in which all members of the school community demonstrate respect and civility.
- Understand students have the right to be treated in a manner consistent with their gender identity and to be free from any form of discipline, harassment, or discrimination based on their gender identity or gender expression.
- Advocate for equal rights and access to free, appropriate public education for all youth, in which students are not stigmatized or isolated based on their housing status, disability, foster care, special education status, mental health, or any other exceptionality or special need.
- Recognize the strengths of students with disabilities as well as their challenges and provide best practices and current research in supporting their academic, career, and social/emotional needs.

School counselors involved in evaluation, assessment, and interpretation:

- Use only valid and reliable tests and assessments with concern for bias and cultural sensitivity.
- Consider the student's developmental age, language skills, and level of competence when determining the appropriateness of an assessment.
- Provide interpretation of the nature, purposes, results, and potential

impact of assessment/evaluation measures in language the students and parents/guardians can understand.

- Use caution when utilizing assessment techniques, making evaluations, and interpreting the performance of populations not represented in the norm group on which an instrument is standardized.
- Conduct school counseling program assessments to determine the effectiveness of activities supporting students' academic, career, and social/emotional development through accountability measures, especially examining efforts to close information, opportunity, and attainment gaps.

School counselors fostering technical and digital citizenship must "advocate for equal access to technology for all students."

Responsibilities to Parents/Guardians, School, and Self

School counselors demonstrating responsibilities to parents/guardians:

- Are culturally competent and sensitive to diversity among families.
- Recognize that all parents/guardians, custodial and noncustodial, are vested with certain rights and responsibilities for their children's welfare by virtue of their role and according to law.

School counselors demonstrating responsibilities to the school "advocate for equitable school counseling program policies and practices for all students and stakeholders." They:

- Strive to use translators who have been vetted or reviewed and bilingual/multilingual school counseling program materials representing languages used by families in the school community.
- Affirm the abilities of and advocate for the learning needs of all students. School counselors support the provision of appropriate accommodations and accessibility. Promote cultural competence to help create a safer more inclusive school environment. Promote equity and access for all students through the use of community resources.
- Use culturally inclusive language in all forms of communication

A school counselor's responsibilities to self include:

- Monitoring and expanding personal multicultural and social-justice advocacy awareness, knowledge, and skills to be an effective culturally competent school counselor.
- Understanding how prejudice, privilege, and various forms of oppression based on ethnicity, racial identity, age, economic status,

abilities/disabilities, language, immigration status, sexual orientation, gender, gender identity expression, family type, religious/ spiritual identity, appearance, and living situations (e.g., foster care, homelessness, incarceration) affect students and stakeholders.
• Refraining from refusing services to students based solely on the school counselor's personally held beliefs or values rooted in one's religion, culture, or ethnicity. School counselors respect the diversity of students and seek training and supervision when prejudice or biases interfere with providing comprehensive services to all students.
• Working toward a school climate that embraces diversity and promotes academic, career, and social/emotional development for all students.

School Counselor Administrators/Supervisors – N/A

School Counseling Intern Site Supervisors

School counselors who serve as field/intern supervisors "are culturally competent and consider cultural factors that may have an impact on the supervisory relationship."

Maintenance of standards: There is no explicit cultural discussion.

Ethical decision-making: There is no explicit cultural discussion.

The lack of cultural discussions around maintaining standards and ethical decision-making stands out the most. Additional critiques are based on both the ASCA and ACA Ethical standards (2016 and 2005, respectively) are summarized in the table below for further consideration. The third column, which is incomplete, offers the reader an opportunity to write their ideas (Table 9.1).

Ethical Case for Reflection: Who Holds the Key to Gender Identity and Gender Expression?

Description: A local school district, named Old County Schools (OCS), has a policy that requires all faculty and students, regardless of their beliefs about biological sex and gender, to use the pronouns that students demand even if this contradicts their biological sex. But there are parents/guardians, teachers, and other school staff who have strong beliefs about not using these pronouns. According to some who are in disagreement with this policy, "Teachers shouldn't be forced to promote ideologies that are harmful to their students and that they believe are false, and they certainly shouldn't be silenced from commenting at public meetings."

The quote comes from a legal representative for a teacher who is suing OCS to argue for their freedom of speech and religious choice.

Table 9.1 Ethical Standards Related to Cultural Competency and Critiques

ASCA	ACA	Critique
A.1.f Respect students' and families' values, beliefs, sexual orientation, gender identification/expression, and cultural background and exercise great care to avoid imposing personal beliefs or values rooted in one's religion, culture, or ethnicity.	**A.2.c** Counselors communicate information in ways that are both developmentally and culturally appropriate. Counselors use clear and understandable language when discussing issues related to informed consent. When clients have difficulty understanding the language that counselors use, counselors provide necessary services (e.g., arranging for a qualified interpreter or translator) to ensure comprehension by clients. In collaboration with clients, counselors consider cultural implications of informed consent procedures, and, where possible, counselors adjust their practices accordingly.	*ACA doesn't address disabilities, aging, or children. How does ACA include school counselors when their ethical codes don't include children and adolescents? ASCA does not include the mental illness piece*
A.6.e Refrain from referring students based solely on the school counselor's personal beliefs or values rooted in one's religion, culture, ethnicity, or personal worldview. School counselors maintain the highest respect for student diversity. School counselors should pursue additional training and supervision in areas where they are at risk of imposing their values on students, especially when the school counselor's values are discriminatory in nature. School counselors do not impose their values on students and/or families when making referrals to outside resources for student and/or family support.	**A.4.b** Counselors are aware of – and avoid imposing – their own values, attitudes, beliefs, and behaviors. Counselors respect the diversity of clients, trainees, and research participants and seek training in areas in which they are at risk of imposing their values onto clients, especially when the counselor's values are inconsistent with the client's goals or are discriminatory in nature.	*Accountability is lacking. Where are the professional development opportunities beyond ASCA and ACA?*

A.10.a Strive to contribute to a safe, respectful, nondiscriminatory school environment in which all members of the school community demonstrate respect and civility.	A.11.a If counselors lack the competence to be of professional assistance to clients, they avoid entering or continuing counseling relationships. Counselors are knowledgeable about culturally and clinically appropriate referral resources and suggest these alternatives. If clients decline the suggested referrals, counselors discontinue the relationship.	Who determines an SC or Counselor's ability to create a safe environment? Where does this information about cultural appropriateness come from?
A.10.b Advocate for and collaborate with students to ensure students remain safe at home and at school. A high standard of care includes determining what information is shared with parents/ guardians and when information creates an unsafe environment for students.	A.11.b Counselors refrain from referring prospective and current clients based solely on the counselor's personally held values, attitudes, beliefs, and behaviors. Counselors respect the diversity of clients and seek training in areas in which they are at risk of imposing their values onto clients, especially when the counselor's values are inconsistent with the client's goals or are discriminatory in nature.	When advocating, who initiates this Students/Families or SCs? Who is doing the inviting? Students/ Families or SCs? Who's responsible for training that combats discrimination?
A.10.c Identify resources needed to optimize education.	B.1.a Counselors maintain awareness and sensitivity regarding cultural meanings of confidentiality and privacy. Counselors respect differing views toward disclosure of information. Counselors hold ongoing discussions with clients as to how, when, and with whom information is to be shared.	

(Continued)

Table 9.1 (Continued)

ASCA	ACA	Critique
A.10.d Collaborate with parents/guardians, when appropriate, to establish communication and to ensure students' needs are met.	B.5.b Counselors are sensitive to the cultural diversity of families and respect the inherent rights and responsibilities of parents/guardians regarding the welfare of their children/charges according to the law.	ACA provides more intentionality about "culturally diverse" families
A.10.e Understand students have the right to be treated in a manner consistent with their gender identity and to be free from any form of discipline, harassment, or discrimination based on their gender identity or gender expression.	C.2.a Whereas multicultural counseling competency is required across all counseling specialties, counselors gain knowledge, personal awareness, sensitivity, dispositions, and skills pertinent to being a culturally competent counselor in working with a diverse client population.	The strength of the ASCA statement is reduced by the very words that are meant to liberate: "based on their gender identity or gender expression." Shouldn't all students be treated as individuals and be able to identify and live in a manner that provides mental health and productivity? ASCA's more active approach is appreciated
A.10.f Advocate for the equal right and access to free, appropriate public education for all youth, in which students are not stigmatized or isolated based on their housing status, disability, foster care, special education status, mental health or any other exceptionality or special need.	C.5 Counselors do not condone or engage in discrimination against prospective or current clients, students, employees, supervisees, or research participants based on age, culture, disability, ethnicity, race, religion/spirituality, gender, gender identity, sexual orientation, marital/ partnership status, language preference, socioeconomic status, immigration status, or any basis proscribed by law.	

		Who's responsible for this Professional Development?
A.10.g Recognize the strengths of students with disabilities as well as their challenges and provide best practices and current research in supporting their academic, career and social/emotional needs.	E.5.b Counselors recognize that culture affects the manner in which clients' problems are defined and experienced. Clients' socioeconomic and cultural experiences are considered when diagnosing mental disorders.	
A.13.a Use only valid and reliable tests and assessments with concern for bias and cultural sensitivity.	E.5.c Counselors recognize historical and social prejudices in the misdiagnosis and pathologizing of certain individuals and groups and strive to become aware of and address such biases in themselves or others.	Need more inclusive language.
B.1.d Are culturally competent and sensitive to diversity among families. Recognize that all parents/ guardians, custodial and noncustodial, are vested with certain rights and responsibilities for their children's welfare by virtue of their role and according to law.	E.8 Counselors select and use with caution assessment techniques normed on populations other than that of the client. Counselors recognize the effects of age, color, culture, disability, ethnic group, gender, race, language preference, religion, spirituality, sexual orientation, and socioeconomic status on test administration and interpretation, and they place test results in proper perspective with other relevant factors.	
B.2.m Promote cultural competence to help create a safer more inclusive school environment.	E.9.a When counselors report assessment results, they consider the client's personal and cultural background, the level of the client's understanding of the results, and the impact of the results on the client. In reporting	

(Continued)

Table 9.1 (Continued)

ASCA	ACA	Critique
	assessment results, counselors indicate reservations that exist regarding validity or reliability due to circumstances of the assessment or inappropriateness of the norms for the person tested.	
B.2.o Promote equity and access for all students through the use of community resources.	F.2.b Counseling supervisors are aware of and address the role of multiculturalism/ diversity in the supervisory relationship.	
B.2.p Use culturally inclusive language in all forms of communication.	F.7.c Counselor educators infuse material related to multiculturalism/diversity into all courses and workshops for the development of professional counselors.	*I think this is coming in ASCA.*
B.3.i Monitor and expand personal multicultural and social-justice advocacy awareness, knowledge and skills to be an effective culturally competent school counselor. Understand how prejudice, privilege and various forms of oppression based on ethnicity, racial identity, age, economic status, abilities/disabilities, language, immigration status, sexual orientation, gender identity, gender identity expression, family type, religious/spiritual identity, appearance and living situations (e.g., foster care, homelessness, incarceration) affect students and stakeholders.	F.11.b Counselor educators actively attempt to recruit and retain a diverse student body. Counselor educators demonstrate commitment to multicultural/diversity competence by recognizing and valuing the diverse cultures and types of abilities that students bring to the training experience.	

B.3.j

Refrain from refusing services to students based solely on the school counselor's personally held beliefs or values rooted in one's religion, culture or ethnicity. School counselors respect the diversity of students and seek training and supervision when prejudice or biases interfere with providing comprehensive services to all students.

B.3.k

Work toward a school climate that embraces diversity and promotes academic, career and social/emotional development for all students.

D.d

Are culturally competent and consider cultural factors that may have an impact on the supervisory relationship.

F.11.c

Counselor educators actively infuse multicultural/diversity competency in their training and supervision practices. They actively train students to gain awareness, knowledge, and skills in the competencies of multicultural practice.

This lawsuit came as a result of a veteran teacher's refusal to honor a student's request to use their preferred pronouns. The fight, from the teachers' perspective, is personal and necessary, because they feel like being dismissed from their position as a teacher was unfair as they were holding firm to their religious beliefs. This lawsuit is contentious and essentially a symptom of greater school district discord concerning this topic. In other words, this is not the only conflict the district is dealing with, but one that is deeply contradictory to accepting all youth as they are within the public school. For this particular case, the legal counsel is arguing that "public employees cannot be forced to contradict their core beliefs just to keep a job. Freedom – of speech and religious exercise – includes the freedom not to speak messages against our core beliefs. That's why our lawsuit asks the court to protect the constitutional rights of our clients by immediately halting enforcement of this harmful school district policy." (For anonymity, the news article and page number cannot be cited.)

Furthermore, the council is arguing that faculty and staff who accept a student's request to use their preferred pronouns when addressing them as a way to validate and help them feel included despite their spiritual beliefs, suggests that "they would be forced to communicate a message they believe is false – that gender identity, rather than biological reality, fundamentally shapes and defines who we truly are as humans, that our sex can change, and that a woman who identifies as a man really is a man, and vice versa. But if they refer to students based on their biological sex, they communicate the views they believe – that our sex shapes who we are as humans, that this sex is fixed in each person, and that it cannot be changed, regardless of our feelings or desires."

This case for which OCS is under fire is one example of one specific topic (e.g., religious freedom, freedom of speech) that overlaps with a school counselor's role. SCs work diligently to help all students feel included. SCs are positioned within a school to help faculty and staff understand the developmental needs of children and adolescents. SCs are often called on by school administrators to be mediators between parents/guardians, teachers, and students. Reflect for a moment on the following questions:

1 Where do you personally stand on this issue in particular?
2 Regardless of your values and beliefs, how do you advocate for equity and access within a school that has a policy that suggests teachers' wishes outweigh the students' wishes?
3 When a policy suggests that teachers do not have to honor a student's preferred pronouns due to religious freedom, what impact could this have on equity-focused lessons, programs, and events that you create to foster environments of inclusive excellence?

4 Advocacy is a role that school counselors can take to battle systemic issues (e.g., exclusive policies, procedures, and practices) in schools and school systems. How do you advocate for your students when much of the work is highly politicized?

The above example is about an issue concerning gender identity and gender expression and the interplay with one's religious beliefs/practices. Below, we add to the conversation by focusing on race and culturally sustaining ethical decision-making.

Racial and Culturally Sustaining Ethical Decision-Making

Racial competence and sustainability refer to the skills and attitudes required to develop and maintain healthy cross-racial relationships, notice and analyze racial dynamics, and confront racism in the environment and in oneself. People are not born racially competent. And yet we often do not ask questions that would give us greater insight because we fear we could expose our gaps in racial aptitude. Racial competence and sustainability in this case place a hyper-focus on race, as this is one of the most anxiety-laden concepts in our society. Whereas, broadly speaking, cultural competence and skills can be summed up as knowing oneself, being open to gaining an understanding of others, developing relational skills (e.g., attentive listening, reflection of feelings, content, and process), accepting and valuing others' beliefs and behaviors, and an openness to learning new things about self and others.

School counselors must develop skills to interact and communicate with students, families, and staff from a variety of cultures with a myriad of cultural and linguistic variables, and should be able to communicate appropriately, both verbally and non-verbally, in each culturally different context (Louw, 2016). Does this imply that school counselors must be able to speak all languages represented within one's school? This seems impossible; however, knowing the different languages spoken and being able to provide translation services for written material, offering a professional translator during school parent or guardian/teacher conferences is important. Without this support, it would be unethical to facilitate a meeting. While school counselors are not necessarily responsible for providing these types of services, school counselors in partnership with school administrators can stand in the gap for parents and/or guardians and advocate to ensure they get the support needed to help their children thrive in school.

Partnering with school administrators to strategize how to appropriately foster inclusive and equitable environments could lead to more successful outcomes. Alternatively, failing to align with school administrators when promoting equitable educational opportunities might lead to difficult legal battles, unwanted media coverage, or even job loss (Stone, 2022).

For the sake of this discussion, racially and culturally sustaining ethical decision-making is a complex process that occurs when encountering minor or complicated professional issues whereby race, explicitly or covertly, is at play. Generally, ethical decision-making requires one to be able to be aware of the foci, have a keen sense of judgment, and have clear thinking to make choices. However, we posit racially and culturally sustaining ethical decision-making must be intentional because the ethical guides established many years ago did not center on race and cultural sustainability. We learn in our master's training program when taking the ethics course that underlying ethical principles that lay the foundation for fostering healthy relationships, work environments, and clinical settings, are *respect for autonomy, beneficence, nonmaleficence,* and *justice.* Justice, in this case, is referring to fairness. However, there is ongoing evidence that our society, schools included, has not embedded racial and culturally sustainable ethical decision-making when it comes to Black and Brown communities.

Therefore, an equity-focused school counselor will need to be savvy. Below is an outline of a model that lacks an intentional look at race and culture. The themes and steps that have been identified to facilitate the process of making decisions to resolve ethical dilemmas are a great guide. When reviewing this guide, think about areas for improvement when using a lens that is inclusive, equitable, and truly affording fair treatment to all students, families, and staff. The general model provided below builds on the work of Johnson (2020). The themes and steps include:

- Describing as many factors about the situation as possible – who the players are and what the context is;
- Identifying and gathering relevant information;
- Identifying relevant ethical issues and possible violations;
- Identifying possible courses of action;
- Consulting with others to examine and study the impact of each action; and
- Choosing a plan of action, and implementing that plan.

The information-gathering aspect of the decision-making process can be time-consuming and very frustrating as it is difficult to decipher what is true, false, or simply a misunderstanding. However, there are more challenges and difficult answers to contend with. For instance, it is important to acknowledge the unique intersections of identity and the power differential among all players involved.

Ethical Decision-Making to Ensure Equity and Justice is Maintained

School counselors will encounter difficult encounters or hear about complex situations that warrant tough decisions around equity and access, especially for Black and Brown students. Brown and Armstrong (2022) discovered that most of the participating school counselors in their study believed they were trained in the use of ethical decision-making models; however, there was consistency in the models that they discussed. One very common and user-friendly model is Solutions To Ethical Problems in Schools (STEPS; Stone, 2017). STEPS is included in its entirety within the Ethical Standards for School Counselors (ASCA, 2016). This model uses nine steps, and it was developed to include developmental issues and parental rights in the ethical decision-making process (Brown & Armstrong, 2022; Stone, 2017). While this model is clearly spelled out, the onus is on the school counselor to practice from a racial and culturally sustaining ethical perspective.

However, the research suggested that within Brown and Armstrong's study, when school counselors were faced with an ethical decision that appeared to have cultural implications that extended beyond their competence, they were less likely to consult with someone deemed a cultural expert. Furthermore, less than 20% of school counselors in the study sought specific culturally appropriate and sustaining assistance. School counselors, like all helping professionals, must be intentional about navigating ethical dilemmas when providing services that foster racial and cultural sustainability within school environments. School counselors need to be aware of the appropriate ethical codes and standards, but they will also need to be brave when engaging in ethical decision-making postures informed by their lens (philosophy, intersections of identity, experiences, values, and upbringing). These same school counselors must also be bold in seeking help to ensure appropriate resolutions to ethical dilemmas, especially when the situations warrant help from school leaders and cultural brokers, to avoid larger problems manifesting (Stone, 2022).

Summary

The following essentially sums up important considerations for making ethical decisions in the face of difficulties – decisions that honor all students and families being served no matter their race, gender, class, and so forth.

First, effective communication is imperative. The goal is to gain a deep understanding of each individual and family involved, their backgrounds, and their beliefs. Next, the school counselor, in concert with administrators, other counselors, and cultural brokers, can choose paths that address stakeholders' needs effectively and critically. Students and families should be able to function in a space that accepts their autonomy, respects their cultural dispositions, and values community. Having a clearer understanding of basic decision-making models and applying one's growing culturally sustaining school counseling ethical practice is a step in the right direction.

Key Takeaways

1 School counselors must be prepared to help children and adolescents navigate difficult life situations, in concert with families.
2 School counselors must make tough decisions in consultation with others.
3 School counselors must remember that families are more invested in their students' success than the school system is.
4 Institutional Racism (e.g., oversight, omission, exclusion) continues to exist in seminal guiding documents within the Counseling and School Counseling profession.

Chapter Application

1 Consider how you can reexamine disproportionality in schools and how you are upholding your ethical standards. What are your observations? What do you think we are missing? Where do you feel the field is going?
2 How will you handle your ethical duty to examine disproportionality in special education and exclusionary discipline?
3 What is one specific area you can target at your school that would shed light on racism? Where do you start this examination?
4 Ethical decision-making skills are informed by your lens (philosophy, intersections of identity, experiences, values, and upbringing). Describe the way in which your lens might impact your ethical decisions.

References

American Counseling Association. (2005). *ACA code of ethics*. Alexandria, VA: Author.
American School Counselor Association (ASCA)-(2016). *ASCA ethical standards for school counselors*. ASCA. https://www.schoolcounselor.org/asca/media/asca /Ethics/EthicalStandards2016.pdf
Atkins, R., & Oglesby, A. (2018). *Interrupting racism: Equity and social justice in school counseling*. Routledge.
Brown, T. A., & Armstrong, S. A. (2022). Use of ethical decision-making Models among school counselors. *Journal of Professional Counseling: Practice, Theory & Research*, 1–12.

Council for Accreditation of Counseling and Related Educational Programs. (2016). *CACREP accreditation manual*. Alexandria, VA: Author.

Johnson, E. S. (2020). Ethical decision-making in educational leadership. *Handbook on Promoting Social Justice in Education*, 785–802.

Louw, B. (2016). Cultural competence and ethical decision making for health care professionals. *Humanities and Social Sciences, 4*, 41–52. 10.11648/j.hss.s.201604 0201.17

Stone, C. (2017). *School counseling principles: Ethics and law* (4th ed.). American School Counselor Association.

Stone, C. (2022). School administrators and school counselors' legal and ethical alliance. *Professional School Counseling, 26*(1c), 2156759X221134668.

Chapter 10

The Intersection of Technology, Crises, and Future Directions

Key Terms (See Chapter 1)
Intersectionality, Racism, Racial Stratification

Author Narrative: Sam Steen

I have some very mixed feelings about technology. I recall being a young boy in the 1980s, having to "code" my own video games, which resulted in a few minutes of great fun after a painstaking amount of trial and error. I recall graduating from high school in 1993 and writing my first email using the world wide web to a friend who was already attending college. This process was quite different than it is now. Receiving a response from my friend usually took a couple of weeks. The novelty of the world wide web gave me the insight that this technology would become a really big deal one day. However, the pace in the late 1990s caused me to no longer want to be a part of new technology trends, in particular, because they seemed to die as soon as something more efficient or more appealing came along. Things were moving too fast and I could not keep up. So, I made a choice right after the Y2K scare – which you may or may not recall was the anticipation of a worldwide computer shutdown from widespread glitches and coding errors related to the year 2000, and the formatting of the digits that were expected to turn to zero and cause massive chaos – to maintain an "old school" perspective and avoid things like Myspace, Facebook, and Pinterest initially. Moving on, Instagram, Twitter, TikTok, and the ones that have since come and gone were not of interest to me at all. I adopted this apathy with engaging social media early on because of the slight trauma (loosely defined) that I experienced in the year 2000, which also was during my first year as a full-time school counselor.

Ironically, my passive affection for technology in a world where more data is created in one day than at any other point in history (in 2020, 1.7MB of data was created every second for every person on earth) was

DOI: 10.4324/9781003226253-12

easy to maintain during the Covid-19 pandemic. However, I have been challenged to reignite a relationship with technology and to set boundaries by using it only as a tool to meet important needs in my personal and professional endeavors.

The writing of this chapter necessitated looking at the most current literature on this topic within the school counseling context. Interestingly, only a few items emerged. After reviewing the articles that I did find, I began to wonder whether I needed to look beyond traditional peer-reviewed and scholarly articles to more current, contemporary, and fast-moving outlets. When I consulted with a colleague who specializes in educational policy and directs a research center at a Research Intensive University, they recommended that I use the following sites to explore contemporary issues within education. For this chapter, I used the few articles I found in traditional scholarly search as well as the following websites:

Education Week (aka EdWeek): http://www.edweek.org/
Chalkbeat: https://chalkbeat.org/
The 74: https://www.the74million.org/

Content

Confidentiality within cyberspaces is also an emerging area of concern. The world will continue to encounter crises of all kinds (e.g., CPS reports, suicidality, natural and manmade disasters) and technological advances will help us all as there are "a lot of opportunities but also limitations to the well-being and safety of kids." The Netflix film *Social Dilemma* highlights this phenomenon. While acknowledging and working through milestones and important school transitions such as preschool to kindergarten, fifth to sixth grade, and senior year to graduation are general considerations during these important points of a student's educational career, the research on the integration of technology into academic, social-emotional, and career outcomes is minuscule. In addition to milestones, extracurricular activities including college acceptance, homecoming, prom, college/career fairs, and so forth could be more fully experienced with technological support. For example, technology (e.g., virtual celebrations) was used to help students participate in ceremonies during the Covid-19 pandemic. In some ways, awareness in the technology arena is particularly needed in public schools. Outside of public schools, we can likely look to the burgeoning numbers of online K–12 schools as a source of useful and innovative information.

Computer and Web-Based Asynchronous Tools to Engage Students

The tools that students can use to engage the world around them are endless. Cell phones, watches, and iPads are typical. Within public and independent schools, laptops are the most common, and desktops are still used to manage large amounts of quantitative and qualitative research data. Regarding software, a few options, including Zoom, Webex, Cisco, and Teams offer connections. Research software includes the Statistical Package for Social Sciences (SPSS), which is essentially a statistical software package created by IBM for managing small and large-scale data, advanced analytics, multivariate analysis, criminal investigation, and business acumen. Another example is NVivo, a qualitative data analysis technology software package that aims to provide researchers with strategies to organize, analyze, dig deeper, and gain clarity on categories of information that at first glance may seem unrelated. The point is, there is no shortage of tools on the market to help with research and practice.

Technology makes it possible to maintain a consistent connection with others and this has become most evident during the ongoing COVID-19 pandemic. It is likely that since the onset of the COVID-19 pandemic, technology knowledge and skills have improved for all. Some literature suggests that school counselors must continue to engage in professional development that offers strategies to integrate online tools within their professional identities in order to make substantial contributions to the communities being served (Mason et al., 2019). As I think about the future, it is not clear how many in-person interactions will remain. Virtual education is here to stay. With this on the horizon, what would experts and laypeople alike suggest as the minimal amount of in-person interaction needed? More recently, the authors have engaged in dialogue about how to deliver instruction in a way that mitigates and overcomes distractions that were less prevalent when meeting in classrooms together as opposed to virtual class meetings. These subtle and obvious deterrents are converging with the online classroom because we all join from different environments and have different comfort levels when engaging behind a computer screen.

In consultation with a newly minted school counseling practitioner in the field, the following questions were posed:

- What computer and web-based asynchronous tools do you use to engage Black/Brown students?
- What outcomes or feedback have you received from web-based interventions used to help Black/Brown children and adolescents in school settings?

- What gaps between research and practice in the effectiveness and application of technology do you see from your vantage point as a practitioner?
- What are some benefits of infusing technology into school counseling programs?
- Describe an instance when you noticed a lack of racial and cultural representation in research or practice for Black/Brown children.
- Your ideas or hunches about the future in light of rapidly changing technologies, crises, or demographics in schools.

Here is a summary of the responses below:

Computer and Web-Based Asynchronous Tools

- Naviance

  - Assessments for self-discovery: StrengthsExplorer, Career Interest Profiler, Career Cluster Finder, AchieveWorks Skills, AchieveWorks Personality, AchieveWorks Learning & Productivity, & AchieveWorks Intelligences

    - I use StrengthsExplorer and Career Cluster Finder

  - Students input SMART goals into the database & can track and monitor alongside staff
  - Students use Naviance database to find/research different careers/ colleges

- SIS StudentVue

  - Students can see grades, attendance, test scores, report cards, schedules, etc.

- Schoology

  - Counselors post resources and important messages (e.g., crisis hotline information, academic advising information)

- GoogleForms

  - Use for pre/post surveys
  - Use for escape room challenges

- GoogleSlides

  - Vision boards
  - Anything that used to be a worksheet

- GoogleSheets

  - Goal-tracking in small groups – each student has a line where they track progress and can see other group member's progress
  - Individual goal tracking

- YouTube (etc.) for engaging videos, calm-down videos (e.g., cute puppies), countdown timers, ambiance
- Zoom for meetings, large events, groups
- PearDeck so students can engage with material whether they're at school or home
- Student emails for communications
- Headspace is free for educators – a meditation app with guided meditations

Outcomes, Feedback, and Gaps

- Students seem to be more engaged, as they can work at their unique pace
- Eliminates situations in which students forget their worksheets at home, lose them, etc.
- Technology is faulty – students don't charge their devices, internet outages, etc.
- School districts limit the tech/online resources you're permitted to use
- A lot of great online curricula/resources/tools are costly
- Certain activities/learning are best done with paper/pencil
- Harder to tell how students are doing when in large groups
- Certain students find working on tech devices to be inherently distracting

Benefits

- Increased reach/equity – more people can access services, resources, and important communications

  - Example: offering to stream/record a Parent Info Night for those who cannot attend
  - Posting lessons online
  - Easier to translate into different languages
  - Closed captioning options

- Built-in data tracking and ease of storing data – saving time
- Aligns practice with the reality of today's world by utilizing a modality most students are comfortable with

Ideas for the future

- Perhaps a shift towards more creative outlets for students showing understanding/mastery to ensure authentic work (ChatGPT)
  - i.e., project-based
- All schools are moving towards every student having a school-assigned computer, iPad, Chromebook, etc.
- Increased use of technology for goal-tracking and journaling

Activity

As you review this summary of ideas, feedback, benefits, and future areas of exploration, what is standing out to you? When you reflect more explicitly on how to include Black and Brown students in this discussion, what ideas emerge? Are there any particular areas of concern that you would raise? To what extent can technology assist in leveling the playing field by creating equitable opportunities for all? How will you maintain technological competency to ensure you use technology for the good of all your students and families? What strategies will you use to communicate to others the benefits and pitfalls that technological advances can create?

Crises

The United States continues to experience an unprecedented awareness of overt racism that was most vividly displayed during the beginning of the COVID-19 pandemic in the form of police brutality. At the point of this writing, media outlets continue to illustrate daily how Covid-19 and its lethal grip is lingering, and in addition to the aforementioned police brutality are ongoing acts of White supremacist displays of hate (e.g., blatant, violent, disruptive disregard for our nation's capital), a myriad of racial inequities within schools exacerbated by the interactions that often occur in cyberspace (e.g., viral TikTok snippets of reenactments of slave auctions), and frequent acts of racially motivated gun violence regularly incited by followers encouraging this violence (e.g., a wide range of Twitter hashtags). These examples of ongoing atrocities are now frequently captured by various forms of technology and blasted on social media. The student's voice is missing from this conversation.

Aside from a pandemic, other potential crises could include anything from natural weather disasters, terrorism threats, public domestic violence, etc. School counselors will need to understand that life transitions, grief, loss, resiliency, and opportunity apply at all times for all people. Crises lead to plenty of changes – those at the initial moment and those that are long-term and experienced during the aftermath.

I (Sam) recall being a first-time school counselor in a new school when the September 11, 2001 attack took place. In addition, a sniper on the loose had an impact on the entire school district and surrounding community later that same year. I was not prepared for these events, but looking back, I recommend the following:

1 Know your school district's policy and your school's plan regarding domestic threats (e.g., active shooter, bomb threats, arson, etc.);
2 Have a personal escape plan in the event that a life-or-death situation occurs;
3 Keep your necessary items with you at all times (e.g., cell phone, car keys, purse, etc);
4 Keep a few non-perishable food and drink items on hand and; and
5 Try to park in the same area so that if/when you are permitted to leave the premises you can find your car quickly.

The technology that exists now and in the coming years will continue to influence every aspect of our society. It was predicted earlier this decade; i.e., 2012, that themes not limited to violence, globalization, wellness, class, and neuroscience will emerge (Studer, 2014). At the time of this writing, more than a decade later, those themes are evident. Mental health and wellness can be seen front and center; the connection between mind and body is gaining momentum, and there remains no shortage of gun violence, war, poverty, and racism. While racism was not predicted as a theme, no one can dismiss the prevalence of racism and its emotional toll. To illustrate, the police brutality briefly described below has become another historical marker of racism displayed in our society, likely because the incident was readily available for viewing. Also, with mandates to shelter in place, more people were at home and consuming social media. It is difficult to debate the fact that racism started within this country nearly 400 years ago when this country began, based on the realities of slavery; however, the video of a White police officer murdering George Perry Floyd Jr, a Black man gasping for air to save his life, was an awakening for many who previously had a difficult time acknowledging or accepting that racism persists and is endemic. To make matters worse, the convicted White police officer received only 22.5 years for Mr. Floyd's death, although the prosecutors sought 30 years for this heinous crime. Unfortunately, this particular display of overt, physical, and cruel expression of racism is just another deadly and violent image we have to contend with. Technology helps to uncover and highlight the racial discord and disharmony that has been embedded within our society since its inception. However, the artificial intelligence associated with technology is not race-neutral, meaning that those responsible for creating the tools and applications must be intentional about ensuring this far-reaching platform is inclusive (Benjamin, 2019). In addition, the users of the tools must also be intentional so that the interactions cultivated by the technology facilitate the potential of those working with our students to counter the racism embedded throughout every aspect of our society.

Technological Opportunities

Racial disparities are highlighted by the emerging evidence that the COVID-19 pandemic has worsened mental health symptoms for Black and Brown communities, deemed the most vulnerable (Oesterle et al., 2020). While both COVID-19 and various forms of racism continue, we believe that school counselors can use their skills either for healing or to perpetuate more harm. We believe that group counseling in particular emerged as a legitimate virtual counseling practice to serve those who were unwilling or unable to participate face-to-face. The pandemic made it impossible to meet in person for several months, and during this time folks living in rural communities or areas where counseling centers or clinical mental health resources were less prevalent benefited from the burgeoning online groups. Such groups became a valuable resource to many (Steen et al., 2023).

As we write this text, the impact of technology continues to explode. Here we provide two illustrations. One is the use of body cameras by the police force. In recent years and based on ongoing police brutality, citizens demanded that police officers wear cameras to record the interactions that the state was having with the people to ensure fair, equitable, and consistent enforcement of the law. In particular, there remain concerns that there are vast discrepancies in how racially minoritized people are treated, and video footage captured continually may expose and lessen these occurrences. Unfortunately, while more footage is captured, there does not seem to be fewer atrocities. For instance, early in the year 2023, five Black Memphis police officers' body camera footage was released across the globe, exposing the brutal beating and kidnapping of Tyre Nichols, a 29-year-old Black man, who was stopped for a traffic violation. Nearly three days later, he succumbed to his injuries and died in the hospital. This type of crisis – essentially the state's violence against unarmed Black and Brown people – has become so common that the same lawyer who represented the families of Michael Brown, Breonna Taylor, and George Floyd (mentioned above) was retained by the Nichols family. Furthermore, this case is so public that the local officials, the FBI, and the U.S. Department of Justice intervened.

Another, less cruel, example of the technological explosion that is well underway is summed up as the growing influence across our society of artificial intelligence. For example, ChatGPT, Perplexity AI, and the AI search engine you.com are released as open-access technology and are currently free to use. These natural language processing tools powered by artificial intelligence technology are able to:

• Facilitate human-like discussions and debates with people who are no longer living;
• Write email messages;
• Create essays;
• Develop poetry;
• Answer questions; and
• Generate lines of code based on prompts put in by the user.

On the one hand, what an exciting time for those intimately involved with the latest technology that enhances the lives of us all. Within school settings, this type of technology could make classrooms more engaging and enjoyable. On the other hand, is the fear of a growing digital divide within school settings or between those with the means to harness and use the technology versus those who may not have access to the tools to engage in a meaningful and productive manner. In particular, cheating and plagiarism are real concerns. Furthermore, the reality is that these types of artificial intelligence can synthesize so much material so quickly that they compromise financial security and safety, and make many people vulnerable to personal or professional exploitations. This type of artificial intelligence was released worldwide at the end of 2022. There will continue to be more development in this arena, and wonderful and exciting happenings will likely unfold. However, the reality of the racial biases embedded within our society could allow this new game-changing phase of technology to perpetuate racism and discrimination. As a school counselor, your work will be influenced by these technological advances. Therefore, it will be important for you to be firm in your own personal beliefs and convictions to stand up against both silent racism and the more covert racism embedded within various aspects of our society and school settings.

Specific Interventions and Technological Opportunities

We take this opportunity to review intersectionality and to challenge readers to reflect on their own intersections of identity and the unique ecological contexts currently being experienced as overt acts of racism and hatred persist. In many ways, counseling services offered in-person or online are not exempt from the potential for great health or great harm that can come when people from different backgrounds are encouraged to speak their truth. In all clinical interactions, ethical principles must be followed. Creating clinical environments that celebrate and honor the voices of all is implied within professional helping professions' codes of ethics, such as the American Counseling Association (ACA), but these guides are not always easily operationalized with cultural sustainability in mind. We discuss the discrepancies and opportunities for school counselors who accept leadership positions to engage in an ethical practice that is fair and just for all in Chapter 9. Take a look at the table below, which provides summaries of the ASCA Ethical Guidelines and ACA Ethical Codes addressing the use of technology to form relationships, foster social justice, administer surveys, and (generally speaking) supervision. Following this table, think about how the guidelines may help or hinder you in your future work as a school counselor (Table 10.1).

Technology and Social Media are Here to Stay

It is apparent from the guidelines above that this document and others like it do not provide all the answers. See Chapter 9 for more details. However, students are engaging in the use of technology, particularly social media. Take a look at the following data shared by a small school in the Northeast, which was soliciting help to eliminate the racial, gender, and political discrimination they were facing. This question was posed to the students, and the data they shared follows:

Question - In your honest opinion, how many hours do you spend on social media, on average, each day during the school week?

Less than 1 hour		54	10.5%
Between 1–2 hours		138	25.8%
Between 2–3 hours		146	27.3%
Between 3–4 hours		108	20.2%
Between 4–5 hours		54	10.1%
More than 5 hours		32	6.0%
	Total Students	534	2.6 hrs average

Weekly Social Media Usage

What can school counselors do about the amount of time their students are spending online? If this time-consuming activity was filled with positive outcomes only, one might argue there is no problem. The harsh reality is that young people and adults alike spend more and more time

Table 10.1 ACA and ASCA Ethical Guidelines Integration

Component	Ethical Guidelines	ACA Code of Ethics
[USE Technology to] Communicate with Stakeholders	• Use clear and understandable language (when producing materials that are presented online) • Consider cultural implications (both in the materials and from whoever delivers the information) • Obtain informed consent and explain the voluntary nature of participation (using accessing tools for all families)	A.2.c.; G.2.a.
[USE Technology to] Form Relationships	• Do not engage in [online] counseling relationships with friends/family, where you cannot be objective. [Set boundaries with technology to ensure lines are not blurred] • Work [creatively using technology such as apps and various software] to develop and strengthen relationships with stakeholders from other disciplines (social workers, university professors, district administration) • Develop clear agreements in advance regarding tasks, duties, compensation, etc. (using various multimedia platforms e.g., Google Drive)	A.5.d.; D.1.b.; G.3.b.; G.3.a.; G.5.e.
[USE Technology to] Advocate & Promote Social Justice	• Advocate at individual, group, institutional, and societal levels to address barriers (using relevant technology and tools available) • Maintain awareness and sensitivity regarding cultural meanings of confidentiality and privacy (within cyberspace) • Assess and address your personal biases, privileges, and barriers to forming relationships (using accessible electronic tools, e.g., Google Forms, QR Codes) A.7.a.; B.1.a.	
[USE Technology to] Share Information	• Ensure privacy and confidentiality are maintained by the research team (e.g., student counselor) [especially online] • Inform stakeholders of the research team's existence, composition, and purpose (using social media platforms) • Inform stakeholders of research procedures and outcomes (social media, X [Twitter], briefs, email blasts)	B.3.a.; B.3.b.; G.2.h.

(Continued)

Table 10.1 (Continued)

Component	Ethical Guidelines	ACA Code of Ethics
Technology	• Ensure that technologically administered assessments function properly • When using technology in supervision, ensure counselor supervisors are competent in the modalities, and protect confidentiality • Acknowledge the limitations of confidentiality when using technology • Consider the accessibility to persons with disabilities and/or cultural barriers • Consider the differences in online communication (verbal vs. nonverbal cues)	E.7.c.; F.2.c.; H.2.c.; H.5.d.; H.4.f.

on social media than they ever have before. As we continue to examine how to promote equity within our schools, take a look at the following data points that come from a school similar to the one mentioned above. These students were asked the following question along with the follow-up:

Have you, personally, been affected by experiences of discrimination at school?

			Percent
Yes		122	23.5%
No		398	76.5%
	Total	520	

If yes, on what basis have you, personally, experienced discrimination online from members at your school?

		N	Percent Respondents
1.	Race	48	9.0%
2.	Ethnic origin	12	2.2%
3.	Religion	18	3.4%
4.	Gender identity	24	4.5%
5.	Sexual orientation	36	6.7%
6.	Politics	60	11.2%
7.	Socio-economic status	12	2.2%
8.	Other	34	6.4%
		Total 244	

Face-to-Face and Virtual School Discrimination

Imagine you were a school counselor in this school and you learn that much of the discrimination students were experiencing was *outside* of school but it was reported *within* the school. This is a complicated issue. At times school administrators may want to avoid addressing these issues. However, as noted in Chapter 7, you are well aware of the impact the surrounding community has on the school itself. The point is that schools are breeding grounds for racial, gender, and political discrimination to name a few. The future will continue to see upticks in this type of atrocity, and the school counselor can be deliberate in addressing these concerns, but not in isolation.

In some respects, you may wonder if you could look to the codes of ethics to help out with these challenges. As mentioned before, codes of ethics are guides that can offer structure to maximize our roles. Nonetheless, school counselors are influential individuals in schools and have plenty of free will to function and behave in the way in which they see fit. School counselors must be firm in their beliefs because they will encounter a lot of difficulties and challenges, especially when dismantling the status quo of White supremacy. Technology used by individuals and school counselors must be used to constantly examine who they are and what they are about.

The authors share positionality statements below as a way to stimulate the reader's own understanding and examination of themselves. Following the authors' brief statements, the reader is invited to share aspects of their own identity.

Sam

To illustrate how I show up in terms of my race and culture, consider the following descriptions of my own intersections of identity. First, I am Black. In addition, my Blackness intersects with being heterosexual, cisgender, Christian, able-bodied, and male. Culturally, this identity embodies African American life and also represents ethnicity, spirituality, connectedness, gathering, and sharing in oral traditions. My experiences as a Black male student pursuing higher education (e.g., Undergrad, M.Ed, Ph.D.), as a counselor, and counselor educator over the years have been riddled with a range of micro-insults, microaggressions, barriers, misunderstandings, racial healing, and support. Messages about work ethic and success were received from my parents. My parents and extended family also communicated that engaging in mental health, nurturing a positive self-identity, and functioning with an "I can" attitude could stimulate resiliency that would be needed when transitioning through various developmental stages in life.

Shekila

I identify as a Black Woman who is cisgender and heterosexual. My faith is deeply important to me. My intersecting identities of both my race and gender operate in tandem. My experiences from the K–12 setting to Academia have been a journey that has taught me that ultimately I want to be both successful and well; these two concepts should not be mutually exclusive. I center my work around liberation and believe that my activist identity is at the core of who I am and how I approach my work. I believe fully in the concept of Power With vs. Power Other, striving to lead and support individuals through empowerment and agency.

Amber

I am a Ph.D. Candidate in Education focused on early care and education (ECE) policy at George Mason University. I am a proud native of Columbus, Georgia. After completing my undergraduate education in 2009, I thrived in a labor organizing and policy career throughout the East Coast and DMV area (District of Columbia, Maryland, and Virginia). I am deeply committed to collective policymaking and action to challenge anti-Black structures in schools. My dissertation examines the cultural values and race-related beliefs that motivate African American parents' and African American ECE teachers' shared racial socialization and identity development processes.

I acknowledge that I enter education research influenced by my prior experiences and beliefs about schooling. I have these beliefs based on my own experiences as a Southern-raised African American person who often had to navigate a complex education system in racially isolating or segregated communities. Considering my intersectional identity as an African American female researcher, I appreciate my own African American ancestors' and parents' significance in my early schooling and still do today. I commit to valuing Black children's lives, strengths, and active participation in collaborative and community-engaged research and practices, understanding that promoting justice for them is a win for all children in our schools.

What about you?

Summary

The pace of technology and its application to the field of education is relentless. Technology is here to stay and is a powerful tool for school counselors to use as an instructional strategy and beyond. School counselors can conduct counseling using online platforms and virtual space. Yet, technology is impacting more than just delivery. Technology can help with collaborative planning activities, master scheduling, and expanding access to all types of resources for students and families. School counselors who want to support the needs of their students will not shy away from ongoing technological developments and advances.

Key Takeaways

1 School counselors need to be open to learning how to use technology to engage all students, especially to combat the residual effects of the Covid-19 pandemic.
2 Research examining the impact of technology on important outcomes for all students is sorely needed.
3 Public crises are rampant in regard to Black people and technology is still used to perpetuate systemic racism.
4 The intersection of technology, crises, and racism will continue to impact schools and the students being served.

Chapter Application

1 Consider how you can use social media to promote your school counseling program and the work you do to create environments that are equity-focused. What are some benefits and areas to be concerned about in using this medium? How do you ensure that a focus on student and family strengths is accounted for?
2 What are some things we learned about all children and families that we did not know prior to the pandemic? How can technology be useful in engaging various students' and their families' perspectives?
3 What are some struggles that you anticipate when utilizing technology to deliver data-driven, evidence-based comprehensive school counseling programs?

References

Benjamin, R. (2019). *Race after technology*. MA: Polity Press.
Chalk Beat - https://chalkbeat.org/
Ed Week - https://www.edweek.org/ew/index.htm
Levy, I. P. (2019). Hip-hop and spoken word therapy in urban school counseling. *Professional School Counseling*, *22*(1b), 1–11.
Mason, E. C. M., Griffith, C., & Belser, C. T. (2019). School counselors' use of technology for program Mmanagement. *Professional School Counseling*, *22*, 2156759X1987079.

Oesterle, T. S., Kolla, B., Risma, C. J., Breitinger, S. A., Rakocevic, D. B., Loukianova, L. L., ... & Gold, M. S. (2020, December). Substance use disorders and telehealth in the COVID-19 pandemic era: A new outlook. In *Mayo Clinic Proceedings* (Vol. 95, No. 12, pp. 2709–2718). Elsevier.

Steen, S., Vannatta, R., & Ieva, K. P. (2023). *Introduction to group counseling: A culturally sustaining and inclusive framework.* New York, NY: Springer Publishing.

Studer, J. R. (2014). *The essential school counselor in a changing society.* Sage Publications.

The Social Dilemma. Directed by Jeff Orlowski. Netflix, 2020. 1 hr., 35 min. https://www.netflix.com/watch/81254224?trackId=14170287&tctx=2%2C0%2Cefc43e2c-4d19-4990-bf86-6897163fe2c9-144219916%2Cfe7d956a-e641-4cc1-a793-b6fa-c1ecef56_53131615X3XX1623769684470%2C%2C

The 74 - https://www.the74million.org/

Chapter 11

Conclusion

Authors' Call to Action

Letters From the Authors

Sam

Dear children,

I want you to know that I engage in this fight for justice in educational spaces as a way to guarantee that you all can feel comfortable in your own skin when attending any school (e.g., Pre-k–20 and beyond) anywhere in this country. This passion was instilled in me by my mother. My mother told me directly that I could achieve anything that I set my mind to and I believed her. As a father to all four of you, I would like to let you know too that you can achieve anything in which you have a strong interest and passion. I will continue to strive to provide you with the insight, wisdom, and strategies to successfully navigate your own journeys.

A good colleague and friend, Dr. Michael Hannon, provides a framework for Black fathers across the intersectionality spectrum in his research. My biggest takeaway from his impactful studies is that I have been assigned, spiritually speaking, to provide, protect, and prepare you for the future. This future, though unpredictable, will be better for you in many ways than it has been for your ancestors. At the same time, there are new obstacles and challenges yet to be imagined. I am working diligently to do my part, both personally and professionally, to provide, protect, and prepare you, using my own experiences as a guide. No matter what you face in your life generally speaking and in your educational journeys in particular, I hope that you really come to understand how much I love you and desire for you to live life freely and fully. You are the motivation for me to never give up on this fight for justice in education and I am hopeful that this work will leave a lasting impact that even my great great grandchildren will stand to benefit from in generations to come.

In the meantime, I would like for you to relay a message to educators that you encounter, but especially school counselors if the opportunity

DOI: 10.4324/9781003226253-13

presents itself. Please share with those influential professionals that they *should* continue to make assumptions about you and any other students that they encounter. Tell them to assume that you have the capacity for excellence and brilliance. Tell them that they can express kindness simply by being encouraging and curious about really getting to know you and your unique contributions to this world.

Sincerely, Dad.

Shekila

Students often ask me what led me to the field of school counseling, and my reply is similar each time: to give children what I did not receive myself. I believe every child is a unique person, who is powerful in their own right and deserves to be heard and provided opportunities that lead them to their best self. I was the child that failed Algebra I, and was concerned about passing Geometry in order to graduate high school. I was proud of the 2.4 GPA I finished with. I was told I would amount to nothing and that a four-year institution was beyond my reach and intellectual capacity. Reflecting back, I was not seen. This little dark-skinned black girl, who worked after school, navigated family dynamics and struggled with processing information made it in spite of her educators.

My advocates in a K–12 setting were few and far between, so when I entered the school system as a counselor, I was determined to give my students more than I received. It is a gift to watch a child grow up, to see a young adult finish high school and make life decisions that begin their journey towards adulthood. What a gift it is to be a contributor and a facilitator! Despite the lack of support I received in the school system, I am where I am today because of the opportunities provided to me outside of school by my mother. Her recognition of my potential was the boost I needed to run the race laid out before me. I am forever grateful.

Amber

Dear reader,

I am deeply committed to shared policy-making and action to challenge anti-Black structures in schools. My expertise focuses on cultural values and race-related beliefs that motivate African American parents' and African American early care and education teachers' shared racial socialization and identity development processes. With this in mind, I believe that family engagement can be a powerful means to build trust and goal-oriented relationships, particularly among Black parents and teachers in early care and education settings.

I seek collaboration with researchers, school practitioners, policy leaders, families, and education agencies. I commit to working towards racial equity with colleagues and allies in the field. We must challenge ourselves to do the work of social justice and confront systems of oppression collectively.

Summary

As individuals, we have a role to play when advocating on behalf of our children, families, and schools. Collectively, we can accomplish more than we can alone. However, there are times when, figuratively speaking, choices to engage directly or to flee are presented. During these experiences, it may be very isolating. We encourage you to resist during these times, spend time reflecting on the pain, seeking out family, peer, and supervisor support while dreaming for the future to come. Then get back in the fight.

Key Takeaways

1 While education is not equal for all students, school counselors can make a significant impact in fighting this inequity.
2 School counselors hold positions of privilege and this necessitates an active approach to social justice.
3 Even though systemic racism is still present in our school communities, school counselors who chose to struggle for justice are not alone in these endeavors.

Index

Pages in *italics* refer to figures and pages in **bold** refer to tables.

For Product Safety Concerns and Information please contact our EU
representative GPSR@taylorandfrancis.com
Taylor & Francis Verlag GmbH, Kaufingerstraße 24, 80331 München, Germany